An Illusive Phantom of Hope

A Critique of Reformism

By: Kyle Rearden

Published by Liberty Under Attack Publications

Copyleft Notice

This book is covered by a BipCot NoGovernment License. Re-use and modification is permitted to anyone EXCEPT for governments and the bludgies thereof.

Further Use Permission: Please feel free to use, re-use, distribute, copy, re-print, take credit for, steal, broadcast, mock, hate, quote, misquote, or modify this book in any way you see fit. Sell it, make copies and hand it out at concerts, make t-shirts, print it on flying disks, or do anything else because intellectual property is a State based haven of the weak, the stupid, and those lacking confidence in their own ability.

Looking for your next read or listen?

1. **Adventures in Illinois Law: Witnessing Tyranny Firsthand** by Shane Radliff (Audiobook/Anthology)
2. **Adventures in Illinois Higher Education: Communist Indoctrination** by Shane Radliff (Audiobook/Anthology)
3. **An Illusive Phantom of Hope: A Critique of Reformism** by Kyle Rearden (Audiobook/Anthology)
4. **The Production of Security** by Gustave de Molinari (Audiobook)
5. **Are Cops Constitutional?** by Roger Roots (Audiobook)
6. **Vonu: The Search for Personal Freedom** by Rayo (Audiobook)
7. **Argumentation Ethics: An Anthology** by Hans-Herman Hoppe et al (Anthology)
8. **Just Below The Surface: A Guide to Security Culture** by Kyle Rearden (Paperback/Audiobook)
9. **Sedition, Subversion, and Sabotage, Field Manual No. 1: A Three Part Solution to the State** by Ben Stone (Audiobook)
10. **#agora** by anonymous (Paperback and Kindle)
11. **Vonu: A Strategy for Self-Liberation** by Shane Radliff (Paperback/Audiobook)
12. **Second Realm: Book on Strategy** by Smuggler and XYZ (Paperback)
13. **Vonu: The Search for Personal Freedom** by Rayo (Special Paperback Reprint/Audiobook)
14. **Vonu: The Search for Personal Freedom, Part 2 [Letters From Rayo]** (Paperback)
15. **Going Mobile** by Tom Marshall (Paperback/Audiobook)

Looking for a publisher? Drop us a line:
www.libertyunderattack.com

Table of Contents

Foreword

Fortunately, reformism hasn't been much of a burden to my time and efforts. I voted once at age 19, attended an Overpasses for Obama's Impeachment that same year, and the next year I held an informational protest against the War on Drugs. As far as reformism goes, I've been quite lucky to not have wasted too much of my precious time. But some have not been so lucky. There are a lot of people who believe that their methods are the ones that will work. Whether it is voting, jury nullification, protesting, debating, or running for public office, these folks think that, through their methods, they can institute positive change and minimize the damage that the State inflicts upon its unlucky subjects.

Although their efforts are, more than likely, good intentioned, they are actually having a negative impact on the change they are trying to create.

I have assisted Kyle with this anthology as much as I possibly could have and could not be happier with the result. It is surely the most extensive and comprehensive collection of articles completely debunking every aspect of reformism.

As an anarchist, it's repulsive to see so many people stuck inside this paradigm, that the only way to impact change is to do it by political means. So many people abandon their philosophical principles because they feel there is no other way out.

But no more; anyone who reads this anthology will realize that working inside the system is no way out, and is only giving legitimacy and credibility to the most dangerous superstition. Those who read this will begin to see an actual, realistic way out.

It is my hope that this anthology impacts as many people as it did me. If there is one piece of work that will do it, it is this one.

To paraphrase Albert Jay Nock from his book, Our Enemy, The State, there are the political means and the economic means of making money. Too many people who claim to want freedom, want to use the political means of making money, and the results have shown that this is not possible.

The answer to reformism, is direct action.

Shane Radliff

Bloomington, IL

Liberty Under Attack

Should You Avoid the News?

[July 1st, 2013]

Throughout history, there have been individuals who had a vested interest in whipping up hysteria amongst the domestic population. By gaining oligopolistic control of the means of communication, these con artists now have the ability to manipulate the populace into whatever direction they should so wish. Despite efforts to circumvent this control, it would unfortunately seem to be the case that a related breed of confidence men do the same thing against American dissidents by pretending to be one of us, all the while directing us down paths that are either ineffectual or counter-productive.

In light of the various subversions within the alternative media, the veracity of attempting to exercise the liberty of the press is now brought into question. Although the impetus to circumvent the mainstream media (MSM) is certainly a good one, I am less than impressed with how the Patriot Rockstars have mangled the message of Liberty, to say the least. What needs to be determined is that, considering the Carousel of Carnivores, should American dissidents avoid the news?

Rolf Dobelli's essay, Avoid News: Towards a Healthy News Diet, gives 15 reasons why he thinks the consumption of news is useless and even harmful (many, if not all, of these reasons are also echoed by Martijn Schirp). Briefly, these reasons could be highlighted thusly:

1. News skews risk analysis
2. News is irrelevant
3. News fails to explain the underlying processes
4. News is physiologically harmful
5. News feeds confirmation bias
6. News encourages shallow thinking
7. News is addictive
8. News increases opportunity costs
9. News divorces reputation from achievement
10. News suffers from a lack of verification
11. News forecasts are always wrong
12. News is a venue for corporate bias
13. News reinforces learned helplessness
14. News projects a false sense of caring
15. News kills creativity

Initially, this sounds completely plausible, but perhaps it would be a good exercise of due diligence to really evaluate these claims made by Dobelli and Schirp. As a good friend of mine has incessantly reminded me, "There are always two sides to every story."First, it is important to understand the current playing field by keeping your ears open, lest you be caught unawares of what the Establishment is doing against you. Second, it would be the height of foolishness to limit yourself to one source (even within dissident, alternative media circles), since this only makes you susceptible to the problem of the Six Blind Men and the Elephant. Again, this is why it's imperative to "shop around," as it were, because of corporate and governmental agendas.

It's not as if Dobelli and Schirp were completely wrong, however. Insincere narratives woven together by self-declared intelligensia want to do your thinking for you, instead of providing you with an explanation of the underlying processes at work; all they really can tell you is "that something happened." Shallow thinking is certainly an epidemic of sorts because people don't think (especially considering the effects of Because YouTube Said So...); this is exacerbated by the lack of due diligence (as exemplified by the claims that the Sandy Hook school shooting was somehow a hoax). And predictive forecasts really are always totally wrong.

Yet, there are some, perhaps unwitting, misconceptions promulgated by Dobelli and Schirp. For instance, these claims of physiological harm seem to me to be akin to the reasoning used by peaceful parenting advocates to explain why they abhor spanking (both neglect to mention that exercise, as a form of stress, increases muscle size, and is thus beneficial for healthy growth). Opportunity costs only arise from the lack of self-control, that is, the news junkies' lack of focus is, in fact, a problem of their own making, and thus such opportunity costs are not the fault of the news; otherwise, such an pseudo-justification could be applicable to quite just about anything. You have to keep in mind that news junkies react without thinking; hence, why they usually have pretty bad cases of the victim mentality.

It's not as if the Carousel is innocent of forming their own celebrity culture, given the very existence of the Patriot Rockstars themselves. These Rockstars are also the same individuals responsible for projecting a public image of themselves as "caring" about the principles of Liberty, all the while leading us down the road to perdition. I view this as the quintessential reason to embrace your own folk and the actual people in your life, rather than give any sort of serious credence to the babbling of some self-made pundit. Finally, the news kills curiosity, not creativity; if you're so scared or cynical that you acquiesce to becoming a couch potato, then it's your own damn fault for not following up on leads for those stories that interest you.

A few more observations are in order that neither the MSM nor the Carousel would care to divulge. It would be foolish to underestimate the effectiveness of the prima facie story tactic, that is, a deliberate obfuscation of the facts that leads the consuming audience into a condition that Gary Hunt has called, "befuddlement," which is essentially the marriage between cognitive dissonance and information overload (put another way, there is so much data the audience can't interpret that they eventually throw their hands up in the air and acquiesce to whatever the self-selected pundits choose to promulgate this week). Equally foolhardy would be to ignore the McVeigh Syndrome, which is the "bravery at a distance" usually exhibited by the Rockstars and their sycophants, as demonstrated most recently by their condemnation of the Hutaree Militia.

So, what is one to do? I think it really depends upon your goals. If your aim is to achieve peace of mind by consciously avoiding exposure to sensationalistic garbage, then yes, I would wholeheartedly suggest that you do what Dobelli initially recommends by completely cutting out all news consumption; however, if your goal is to counter the MSM, then what you should be doing instead is looking at all the sides of a story from as many primary sources as possible, before forming a judgment. Obviously, this is quite difficult to do individually, and is best done in a collective effort of some kind, perhaps in the form of a verification clearinghouse.

How is one to apply these suggestions, though? Dobelli advises us to read books, magazines, and trade journals instead, as well as the need to talk to friends and family. The problem with these recommendations is that since the news is time-dependent (unless you're reading an investigative expose), your circle of personal contacts, more likely than not, are getting their information from the very same news services that you are abstaining from in the first place. Perhaps a better avenue is to verify the sources for yourself, and the first steps to doing this in a cooperative manner is the Committee of Digital Correspondence. They are still seeking correspondents, so if you want to write sourced articles for them, they would be happy to publish high-quality reporting.

Ultimately, I have a sinking feeling that most dissidents I've talked with over the years aren't truly interested in tackling the MSM, despite their Reactive Ralphie impressions to the contrary. What comes across clear as day is their desire to simply not be bombarded with corporatist agendas, in which case, I will recommend to them my thoughts as a refinement upon Dobelli's suggestions – cut down on how much time and effort you spend reading, listening, and/or watching the MSM and the Carousel, and instead spend that time writing book reports (like I do), since I think you are much more likely to find sources for the truth in carefully researched (though possibly dated) books, rather than incomplete and misleading news articles, radio broadcasts, or video press releases. Perhaps then you'll start to realize that it's not necessarily the truth, but your own personal liberty, that matters.

Debating Does Not Work

[August 6th, 2012]

We continually hear from various alternative media pundits that in order to "take our country back," we need to win the infowar by verbally bludgeoning the mainline public into seeing through the fog. One such method for doing this is by engaging in fruitless arguing over specific issues, even when there is a fundamental difference in worldviews. All too often this results in needless confusion, destructive balkanization, and mental exhaustion.

Regardless of whether it occurs over email lists, forum boards, comment threads, video responses, live Internet radio streams, or even face-to-face meetings, debating with another individual with whom you disagree on fundamentals is literally retarded. It is very unlikely you will persuade someone to much of anything, all the while it is very likely you will end up pissing off everyone, yourself included. Had you simply inquired into their ideology, that by itself should answer most of your potential questions; unless you are asking clarifying questions (without expressing your own thoughts) on a given subject with the goal of trying to more fully understand their position, then any sort of discourse is going to be patently unproductive for all participants involved.

If you think I am exaggerating (or just being plain too cynical), it would behoove you to notice what happened when those voluntaryists debated some socialists at the Café Libertalia in San Diego two years ago. Keeping in mind that it was a formal debate, my chief criticism of it was not really seeing what exactly was accomplished, if anything. I noticed that once the two debate teams hit an impasse, the entire event began degrading into a combination of repetitive slogans and silly hypotheticals that did anything but clarify where either of them were really coming from (of course, since I understood their respective ideologies beforehand, I more or less knew what was being left out).

Too many times have I observed flame wars on the information superhighway. Everything from spanking young children to public school students ridiculing a bus monitor to how to treat sexual dysfunction has been debated up and down the line without any sort of real conclusion, consensus, or even just plain clarification. Moderators use such tenuous situations to worsen balkanization by playing fast and loose with their site's terms and conditions regarding acceptable behavior by arbitrarily removing one of the parties involved, usually the one they already disagreed with; all such "discussion" of that kind only gives rise to sanctioned bullying.

I found it humorous (in a very macabre way) when Brenda Huffman asserted that political debate is actually healthy; nothing could be further from the truth. Granted, the liberty of free speech is paramount, but the issue here is not that but instead whether reckless "debating" and ridiculous argumentation actually moves the case forward for securing our Liberties. Huffman's sugarcoating of how vociferous political engagement by expelling a gargantuan amount of hot air (that increases carbon footprints, which I am all for) is completely disingenuous. People are pissed off (and rightly so) about the Establishment's increasingly heavy handedness; "fever pitch" debates are symptomatic of an incredibly worsening situation, just as the one the Founders were forced to contend with.

What really gets me is that, at the end of the day, what was truly accomplished? So you have some passionate guys yell (or type quickly) at each other about what seems to be some abstract, opaque phenomena in the eyes of John Q. Public. If the goal was to persuade people and change their minds, how can that be measured? By virtue of the fact that it isn't measured, as well as the emotive drama that necessarily accompanies such "debates," it would seem to suggest that the real motive behind such farcical argumentation is not in what it purported to accomplish, but instead was no more than an exercise in self-aggrandizement.

Even arguing with people who do agree with you on essential concepts is unnecessarily risky, unless you have either the skill or talent for diplomacy. It would be foolhardy to alienate good contacts prematurely; instead, give them some literature and allow them to "convert" themselves. Such interpersonal one-on-one mentoring is actually quite effective, but admittedly, it is nowhere near being as sexy or dramatic as getting people throwing chairs.

Should You Write a Letter to the Editor?

[May 15ᵗʰ, 2013]

Many activists over the years have suggested to their respective audiences that one of the things they can do to be "engaged" and "active" in the political arena is to write a letter to the editor of a newspaper. Interestingly, they do so flippantly, never evaluating the effectiveness of such a method. Unfortunately, the truth in many situations, such as this one, is quite nuanced.

A wide-spread assumption within various dissident circles is that it is still desirable to use the mainstream media to our advantage, in much the same way a guerrilla feeds off the captured supplies of his imperial enemy. The real question though is, just how effective is this guerrilla infowar tactic? Realize first that there is a very low probability that any letter you write to the editor will end up getting published; and second, even if the paper in question has a pretty wide circulation, how do you measure how many people actually read it?

Any sort of market feedback is more accurate and reliable in the alternative media than anything the lame-stream dinosaur talking bobble heads can provide to you. Modern self-publishing technology now guarantee the availability of the tools needed to exercise the use of the proverbial soapbox, whereas letters to the editor are simply asking for permission to speak. Does only concentrating on activities like blogging, podcasting, and videography unnecessarily limit yourself to a niche market? Sure it possibly can, but at least you know the numbers of hits and views; even then, it is still open for your detractors to comment, unlike the corporate whore papers.

There are also the privacy implications to consider. Benjamin Franklin was able to write letters to the editor of the New England Courant under the alias Silence Dogood, thereby portraying himself as a very opinionated widow, yet he was never once asked "Your papers, please!" James Wesley, Rawles has recommended people to use a pseudonym when writing letters to the editor, since he is concerned about INFOSEC. So, you would think it is relatively easy to do so, given both these historical and contemporary examples, right?

Sadly, such is not at all the case here. Just by concentrating on a smattering of local newspapers here in Austin (as well as different local newspapers in other cities that served as a type of control group), I was able to determine that it is literally impossible to "anonymously" write anything to the editor and expect a fair gamble at getting it published.

Granted, papers are free to publish whatever letters they receive, but what I object to here is the constant "policy" of them either demanding some combination of your legal name, physical or mailing address, and/or telephone number before you are allowed to submit your letter for potential publication, or asking you for these details after they've made the decision to publish your letter, yet still make it only a conditional acceptance as such (depending on the individual newspaper).

If you think I am overreacting to this overtly corporatist behavior, consider what happened to Michael Kuzman back in 1981. He wrote a letter to the editor of a local paper expressing his personal views about (what some would think of as) a controversial political topic. As a direct result of the publication of his letter, the Criminal Investigation Division of the IRS conducted a 4 day surveillance operation on Mr. Kuzman and his family. What crime was he suspected of committing? We will probably never know for sure, but what is crystal clear here is that writing a letter to the editor, especially in the context of exercising political speech (which was supposed to be legally protected by the First Amendment), makes you a target for political persecution, hence the need to be able to publish anonymously, which the mainstream media has now made it virtually impossible to do. Welcome to police state America.

Probably a nearly untouched upon aspect regarding the validity of writing a letter to the editor is, what exactly is the goal here? Is it to win over hearts and minds? Is it a naïve attempt to somehow "recruit" people to join your particular organization? Or is it simply an opportunity for self-aggrandizement? Comparing this with writing your congressman, consider the respective audiences: congressional staff members who shoot back out a standardized form letter, or random people who in all probability are least apathetic, if not outright hostile, to what you have to say. True, those random people are a noticeably larger sampling than just a few congressional staff aides, but at least you can determine the results of such letters (that is, how the congressman voted on particular bills versus pretty much nothing at all). I am not implying anything statist here; I am simply pointing out that the feedback for the government version is much more reliable and accurate than the corporatist flavor (and most importantly, the free market alternative media has the best feedback of all, thus vastly surpassing the other two).

During the constitutional ratification period of the late 1780s, Americans had a reason to care about what was happening around them. They had just won a bloody 7 year war for their independence in order to try something distinctly new, and they didn't want to leave to chance anything that could bollocks it all up. It was at this pivotal time in American history that letters to the editor framed the public discourse, thus determining in many ways how the delegates to the state conventions were to vote on ratification of the federal Constitution. An anthology of these letters in favor of the Constitution were collectively published as The Federalist Papers (it wasn't until much later that those letters published at the time in various newspapers critical of the Constitution were somewhat haphazardly compiled into what eventually became known as The Anti-Federalist Papers). Seeing that such aliases as "Publius" and "Federal Farmer" were used, I sincerely doubt those writers were obliged to reveal their personal identities as a condition of actual (or even likely) publication.

We have lost something very precious to the American experience, that is, the ability to use pen names in writing letters to the editor in order to express politically controversial thoughts. Thankfully, we have the Internet as a tool with which to exercise our liberty of free speech, but we shouldn't have had to rely on it so much. It doesn't negate the fact that the incessant "policy" of the media corporatocracy is to elicit from us our "real" identities as a precondition for publication; such information is, of course, used for profitable data-mining purposes (contrary to what their alleged "privacy policies" may ostensibly say).

So, what can be done as an alternative to writing letters to the editor of a corporatist publication? You could do what many people in the alternative media did back in the '90s before the Internet went big and write a letter to the editor of a newsletter (such as the former American Sentinel or Sobran's). Another option is to treat those editors the same as congressman and simply mail them brightly colored postcards; since it is now common for there to be word limits, you might as well take advantage of the situation and act in accordance with it, for you will not be granted the privilege of writing even half the length of Agrippa's letters. I also recommend writing your own book reports exposing the evils of the Establishment, and this can be accomplished by posting them on discussion forum boards, by blogging, or even by micro-blogging.

Thomas Jefferson once said, "I'd rather have newspapers and no government, than government and no newspapers." While I can appreciate the sentiment, I think even he could understand why I cannot agree with his preference for my own nuanced reasons. At this juncture, I would rather bypass these newspapers (and even the Internet, to some degree) by giving people who live near me locally some literature and allowing them to "convert" themselves, instead of "debating" with them using the soapbox. The Carnival of Distractions has wrought enough damage by wasting valuable human time and energy into ineffective and even counter-productive tasks. I think it is high time for my fellow bloggers to expose them for their misdeeds by writing audio timelines, thereby documenting their foolish talk for those who bother to read! Hopefully, by demonstrating the foolishness of such techniques like writing congressmen or editors much of anything, we can then regroup and begin to ascertain how to more effectively secure our Liberties.

Writing Your Congressman Does Not Work

[May 22nd, 2012]

Most alternative media websites instruct their audiences on how to write to "their" Congressman, all the while pontificating the virtues of its alleged efficacy. Such fallacious advocacy permeates the remnants of the free press, most of whom actually know better, but for some inane reason, persist in recommending to others that they should waste their valuable time and effort on a technique that systematically fails to deliver measureable results in the cause for liberty. Believing in the civic fairy tale that politely requesting a legislator, who imagines himself to be your ruler, to abide by his oath of office through opposing unconstitutional legislation, is just as constructive as thinking that cancer can be inexplicably "reformed."

Legislators are not constitutionally required to accept your mail, much less answer you, or otherwise perform whatever you wish them to do. Just because citizens have a constitutionally recognized ability to petition the government for a redress of grievances does not therefore mean legislators have a corresponding duty to respond back to you. Any responses you receive back from any of them should be considered within the bounds of polite etiquette.

Consider also the difficulty of proportionality experienced by these congresscritters. In 2013, the total United States population of voting age (that is, over 18-years-old), was approximately 243,703,099 people, and the total Texas population of voting age that same year was projected to be 19,518,666 individuals. If you know that the entire United States Congress has only 535 voting members, and that the entire Texas legislature has only 181 voting legislators, then what this means is that the ratios of "representation" can be calculated out to be 1 congresscritter for every 455,519 U.S. citizens, and 1 Texan legislator for every 107,837 Texans.

Obviously, in light of these ratios between legislators and citizens, it becomes literally impossible for every letter received to be answered; thus, an automated process was born. What happens is that the legislative staff categorizes letters into a dichotomous typology of "pro-whatever" and "anti-something," types your name at the top of the pre-written standard form letter, and returns that to you. This is all based on the assumption that the congresscritter's staff got not only the subject matter correct, but also accurately recorded which side of a political issue you were on in the first place. Yup, that's right – it's been well-known by those who have worked inside the legislative branch of government that such "mishaps" as these are all too common.

The truth of the matter is that writing to a politician is, in fact, a purposefully designed confidence trick. You are supposed to emotionally invest yourself in the notion that "your" congresscritter represents your interests, where, truth be told, they just don't give a damn. Every minute spent on the working inside the system in order to change it from within (that is, the political means of making money), is every moment not being spent on doing something actually productive towards making humanity freer.

Contemplate also the implications to your privacy should you ever write a congresscritter. They'll have your mailing address from the envelope, and quite possibly enough information from your letter with which to unjustly profile you as a political undesirable. As long as they don't accuse you of "terrorism," then perhaps writing congresscritters, although it incurs opportunity costs, shouldn't land you in a government dungeon.

Being the good scientist I am, I decided to conduct my own experiment of sorts by writing some congresscritters on two different political issues. In 2013, I opposed both CISPA in the federal Congress and the grandparent access legislation in the Texas legislature. The postcards I sent to the applicable congresscritters, as pictured below, were much less time consuming than if I had written letters and then placed them into envelopes, as well as being much more privacy-friendly.

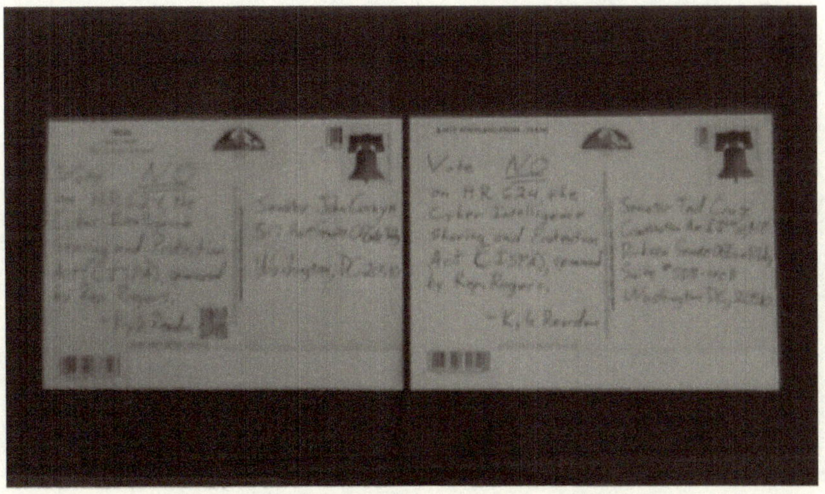

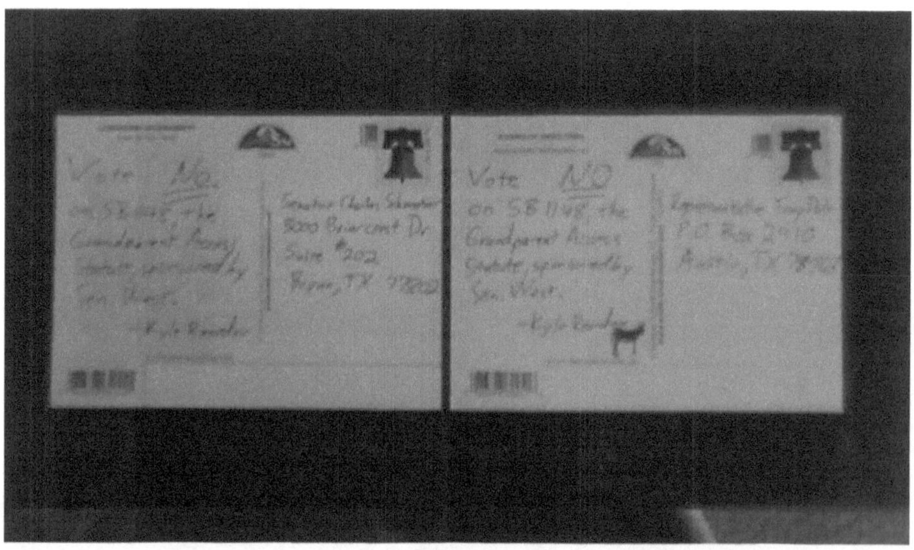

Thankfully, CISPA died in committee, as was the similar fate with the grandparent access statute, yet Fight for the Future has recently warned that CISPA is not dead. I think this shows exactly the problem with writing congresscritters at all – even if your letter is correlated to the fate of a bill, there is nothing preventing the same legislation to be packaged differently and passed into law at a later time. Unless you are willing to dedicate yourself into becoming a watchdog, there is absolutely no way for your average Joe to keep on top of the legislative branch for any American government.

There are, however, some slight exceptions to the historical observation that writing to a congresscritter does not work. They are:

- ❖ If you're a lobbyist
- ❖ If you're a celebrity
- ❖ If you're a massive campaign contributor, or
- ❖ If the congresscritter does not possess the incumbency advantage for the next electoral cycle, which is rare.

For those who can't bear to not write "their" congresscritter, the next best thing is to mimic my example by sending brightly-colored postcards, scrawled with pithy statements either in support of, or opposition to, a particular bill. Better yet would be to ask them stupidly polite questions wherein any real answer would betray the façade of their very "representation." Such uncomfortable questions and any subsequent replies should be published in corporate media newspapers, as well as any alternative media outlets, that care to expose the opportunity costs and hypocritical futility of reformism itself.

Petitioning Does Not Work

[May 11th, 2013]

Reformism is all about working within the system that you have inherited. You follow the rules of that government, no matter how arbitrarily chaotic or conspiratorially despotic they are, in the hope that you can eventually turn it against its own nature, and towards whatever it is that you want instead. Sadly, it is neither guaranteed, nor even probable, that such measures will actually work in achieving your goals.

Petitions are little more than attempts at begging a particular type of government agent, usually a legislator, to please be nice to you and not act as dictatorial as he presumably otherwise would if you had not begged him. In fact, Ballantine's Law Dictionary (3rdedition) defines a petition (in part) as "a formal request in writing addressed to one in a position of authority." Wait a moment…so, even by drafting and sending this type of legal document, the petitioner implicitly recognizes the alleged "au-thor-ity" of the government agent in question. This presents a rather interesting conundrum, for if you chose to not recognize such authority, wouldn't petitioning a legislator either reveal your ineptness, or even worse, deliberate hypocrisy?

The First and Ninth Amendments to the US Constitution state that:

"Congress shall make no law respecting an establishment of religion, or prohibiting the free exercise therefore; or abridging the freedom of speech, or of the press; or the right of the people peaceably to assemble, and to petition the Government for a redress of grievances. [emphasis added]

"The enumeration in the Constitution, of certain rights, shall not be construed to deny or disparage others retained by the people."

Sections 27 & 29 of the Texas Bill of Rights declare that:

"The citizens shall have the right, in a peaceable manner, to assemble together for their common good; and apply to those invested with the powers of government for redress of grievances or other purposes, by petition, address or remonstrance. [emphasis added]

"To guard against transgressions of the high powers herein delegated, we declare that everything in this 'Bill of Rights' is excepted out of the general powers of government, and shall forever remain inviolate, and all laws contrary thereto, or to the following provisions, shall be void."

So, while it is true that you have the liberty to petition the government for a redress of your grievances, what it doesn't mean is that they are obligated to obey your demands or listen to you in any way; in fact, they are at liberty to completely ignore you. The only problem here is that if they do that too often (much at the expense of the common people for the benefit of the wealthy corporatist special interests), the legitimacy of their bond of representation with the population comes into question, which is where we find ourselves today.

Whether it be the federal Congress or your respective state legislatures, legislators have little to no incentive to listen to anything you have to say, much less give you the time of day. As I have mentioned before on the topic of writing your congressman, unless you qualify in one of those exceptional categories (which by default, most people don't), a legislator is not going to take you seriously. The closest "foot-in-the-door" exception would be to become a grassroots lobbyist, but even that too presents both logistical and ethical problems in terms of securing your Liberty. Unless your financial coffers are bursting to the seams from the many donations of liberty-lovers who aren't beholden to corporate special interests, then you might be a serious contender against the professional lobbyists. Otherwise, you'd be better staying home and flushing your Federal Reserve Notes down the toilet (at least that way, you can save yourself the time and aggravation of negotiating with congresscritters).

Why does the alternative media push the use of petitions so hard for nearly everything? I suspect many genuine individuals naively think that if they focus the audiences' attention upon a safe measure for whatever is ailing the body politic this week, then they will be doing them a kindness, even with something that is guaranteed to fail in achieving its stated goals. Ironically, nothing is more cruel that fostering a false hope in the minds of those who truly yearn for their liberty. Some even advocate the use of petitions not for their original purpose in making substantive political change within the government, but as a propaganda tool to grab mainstream media attention. Needless to say, if you require the corporate whore media to spread the message of Liberty, then we might as well pack up all our toys and go home to stay for the rest of our days, because that kind of dependence is not within any sane realm of reality for what we have to deal with in terms of at least trying to shrink this Leviathan we are all suffering under.

Some might be hesitant about filing petitions because of the privacy implications of doing so. Regardless of how any petition is written and delivered, it is still a legal document, and as such the use of aliases or the implementation of other typical INFOSEC measures cannot be used, since everything here has to be done completely aboveboard. Having said that, I don't think it is wise to sign your name onto every petition that vaguely sounds good. It would behoove you to at least read the petition before you sign it, lest you become a foolish stooge in a Mark Dice type petition hoax video.

What has been the track record of petitions thus far? Have they increased or restored anyone's liberty or property? It would seem to be the case that they have fallen through the cracks of modern history by being systematically ignored by those very government agents who have it within their power to act on them, and, it bears repeating, they have no incentive to do so. As Albert Einstein famously quipped, "Insanity is doing the same thing over and over again and expecting a different result."

Online petitions have been all the rage as of late. Following the alleged reelection of Barry Obama, there was a flurry of digital petitions about all sorts of topics, but some of the more noticeable ones centered around the theme of begging the White House to allow their respective state governments to peacefully secede from this highly overrated Union. As you can no doubt probably infer, nothing happened, although some of the older heads within the Patriot Community reasonably speculated that everyone who "signed" one of those digital secession petitions are likely by now to be on some police state watch list somewhere.

Even before the White House digital secession petitions took off, there was an activist group being promoted by the Carnival of Distractions known as Food & Water Watch (FWW). Unfortunately, the "Take Action" page for this organization was nothing anything more active than encouraging their readership to fill in the email contact forms for various single-issue items. While they may have had the best of intentions, I seriously doubt any of those single-issue items are going to be resolved in any manner, despite FWW's previous claims where they tooted their own horn about their previous "victories."

Ultimately, how do we measure the contemporary effectiveness of petitioning the government for a redress of our grievances? Well, as I am sure that it is easier to data-mine and profile digital petitioners, it also makes it easier for any legislative staff to ignore; when contrasted with paper petitions, it is revealed that not only the later affords greater privacy protection, but also a marked increase in (at the very least) the probability that some random staff member will actually read the damn thing. The real trick here though is in getting actual feedback, which is unusually difficult. Generally speaking, you are inherently relying on either receiving a letter back (typically in the form of a standard, totally non-informative letter), or acting as a watch dog by regularly checking up on floor votes in the

Congress. It goes almost without saying that the latter method is the only reliable one that tells you just how effective your petition was, but it requires quite a bit of due diligence in constantly checking the congressional record.

If anyone were actually serious about petitioning the government for a redress of their grievances, the best one I have found for doing so is the You Have Tread on Me – Under One Banner petition. A major drawback of single-issue petitions is that they may appeal to some, but not to others; by contrast, multi-issue petitions are automatically more likely to attract large numbers of signers, and thus have more of an effect. Petitions should also be solution focused in their wording, otherwise they will not be taken to heart and treated seriously. Best of all, the Under One Banner petition is a paper petition, which means you would have to sign it using an actual pen! Not only that, it is also preferable to hand deliver three copies of this petition to "your" congressional Representative and two US Senators each, falling back on snail mail only as a last resort.

At the end of the day though, do petitions actually work? Gauging from previous history, as well as how they have been further bastardized by the onset of these so-called online petitions, I'm just gonna go ahead and say no. Omnibus bills and riders grafted onto unrelated pieces of legislation continue unabated, completely unaffected by pitiful begging to discontinue such practices. Such behavior is firmly entrenched in the District of Criminals, and sadly, in many, if not nearly all, of the state legislatures as well. It would be folly for us to assume this late in the game that it is still possible to put an end to tyrannical government by begging them to be a little nicer to us, even in the context of a support mechanism. At this juncture, nothing less than working outside of the system is going to provide even a modicum of a chance for us to possibly secure our Liberties.

Voting Does Not Work

[June 1ˢᵗ, 2012]

The greatest tyranny is the tyranny of malicious illusion. Endorsing organized coercion by pretending it is somehow voluntary is not just unconscionable, but downright cruel. Deceitfully passing off vice as virtue is the last thing that truly consistent political dissidents would want to risk doing, lest they be discovered to be just as hypocritical as those they intend to defeat.

In order for a Republic to work, the populace must be competent enough to elect representatives to the legislature. Considering the various statistics and research studies suggesting that the majority of Americans are incompetent buffoons (courtesy of the public fool system), this would indicate such a high level of ineptness to the point that these are exactly the type of fools who would easily be conned into supporting a politician through emotional rhetoric instead of based on rational criteria. Other social science research shows that people who lack expertise in a given subject (in this case, politics) are too incompetent to gauge the quality of whether anyone is qualified for public office. Worse, they are so incompetent to the point that they can't even accurately estimate the severity of their own ineptness, always overinflating their performance on various tasks.

Another study revealed that political partisans, when presented with objective facts, will twist those in such a manner as to hang on to those facts that support their preconceived notions while conveniently ignoring the rest of them. According to psychiatrist Scott Peck, there exist only a "fortunate few" who are able to successfully avert this self-delusional trap, and thus possess the best chance of being even somewhat objective. I think it is fair to declare at this point that most American voters are an uneducated, slovenly mob instead of being an enlightened, rational citizenry.

Voter fraud is an all too well-known topic, yet for some idiotic reason, many political dissidents still think they can elect their preferred Messianic figure despite this. Ballot results are relatively easy to forge; electronic voting machines just made the fraud that much easier than the traditional paper ballots, which actually required some "creative accounting" skills to pull off. There have been provable incidents where particular agents of the State don't actually deserve their jobs even according to the government's own rules; thus, the air of legitimacy (which was already incredibly thin) totally evaporates.

Similar to how congressional aides regularly don't correctly record which side of a political issue geographical constituents are on in the first place, it's not that all uncommon for votes to be "misrecorded" either. Regardless of when voting officials actually do record results even halfway accurately, they admittedly keep databases on voting histories (so called "enhanced voter files") with the explicit intention of profiling voters for the next electoral cycle. Everyone who chooses to vote is getting their individual voter files datamined by both the Democrats and the Republicans.

Voting encourages compromise by instilling in the body politic the supposed necessity of selecting between "the lesser of two evils." Besides the fact that the lesser of two evils is still evil, defensive or protest voting only serves to perpetuate the illusion that if you vote "against" a candidate, you're not really voting for his opponent. Such a fallacious notion really belongs in the wasteland of failed ideas, for the history of human experience testifies to the antithesis of that thought.

Downs' Median Voter Theorem narrows the range of options down to a set of strict binary "choices," that are, in fact, so very similar to each other as to be nearly indistinguishable in substance, even though they may seem superficially dissimilar. Any other choices that may be presented from time to time are not given equal weight as the two primary darlings are. The Left-Right Paradigm manipulates the median voter theorem so as to artificially limit the "serious" political candidates to those who are beholden to the dual hegemonic political parties.

The most generous individual vote strength percentage I've ever seen is .0253%, which is attributable to the average UK voter. For Americans, one forum discussion thread centered on the ever-shifting variables of the sample size of eligible voters, the turnout of those voters, and whether the contested area is in a swing state. A figure of .00086% was given, but that was attributed to only those who voted early and often. What I found most revealing was the chap who invented the Voter Power Index admitting that single member plurality voting "is profoundly undemocratic" and "betrays the fundamental principle of democracy – one person, one vote." The point here is that, holding all other variables constant, individual vote strength percentages are so absurdly minuscule as to be essentially inert.

Some would argue that if the voting system were anything other than winner-take-all, then election results would reflect the "will of the people" and thus be truly representational. Typically utilizing a multi-party structure, proportional representation (PR) enacts preference ordering of candidates, so as to eliminate the "wasted vote" syndrome. Despite this, what still wins elections (quantitatively speaking) are dedicated voting blocs, coalitional voting discipline (as in the case of PR), and especially straight-ticket voters. Essentially what happens in PR is that the special interests become the political parties, so instead of the special interests bribing legislators to pass bills that exclusively favor them (which is known as lobbying), they write and pass the bills themselves, despite even open-list PR. The main flaw of proportional representation is that it encourages corporatism even more then single-member plurality voting already does (especially considering Duverger's Law).

Legislators, as the most commonly elected agents of the State, are beholden to their campaign contributors, NOT their geographic constituents (except in rare cases when they are one and the same). The party who throws the most Federal Reserve Notes around will always trump the plebeian civilian schmucks who happen to live in the same area. Once successfully elected, the politician in question now possesses the incumbency advantage, which is a game changer. The rule is to stay in office; the exception is to be beaten.

Most popular electoral media coverage is on the executive branch, not the legislative. This is pretty startling, considering that the legislative branch was the only one that was specifically designed to be representative; it is what makes a Republic of what otherwise would be a military junta, an absolute monarchy, or a Communist dictatorship. Voters have more sway over legislators than the President, but they are told to focus more on something they automatically have less effect over.

Even worse than this is the overemphasis on executive over legislative elections as well as the hyped focus on federal over state-level (or provincial) elections. The fact that a gubernatorial election is considered less newsworthy than the Presidential election is alarming since your Governor is infinitely more important and more accessible to you than the President ever will be. The fact that Congressional elections are considered more important than the state-level legislative elections is appalling, since your state senator (for instance) affects your life more directly than some douchebag US Senator ever will. After all, Minarchism is all about LOCAL government on the smallest scale possible.

Many dissidents have heralded more popular democracy as the antidote for what ails the body politic. What these well-meaning souls fail to realize is that popular voting has proven to lessen our Liberty, especially considering two important historical precedents. The 17th Amendment utterly gutted the purpose of the US Senate as being representatives of their state legislatures to being considered as yet one more US representative. This not only lessened the perceived relevance of the 50 state legislatures, but also mocked the balancing act of federalism. The subsequent gutting of the Electoral College is especially appalling; first, over half of the states in the Union are bound to the popular vote; second, in the non-biding states they are "advisory," but in that case, why should the Electors give a flying flip? They should vote according to their own criteria instead of what the uneducated democratic mob feels like doing at the moment.

Notable alternative media figureheads will occasionally spout the invaluable benefits of "direct democracy" tools. Referenda are promoted as a runaround the legislature by providing an opportunity for the hapless civilians in a local area to vote on a piece of legislation. Recalls are designed to remove a public servant from office before his term ends. The problem with both are that not only do they typically rely on petitions to get started and that during each there is the ever present tyranny of the majority, but also that you are inherently relying on government officials to tally the votes.

Curtis Ellis, the same bloke who invented the concept of "democracy commandos," has made a suggestion that voting must be made compulsory! The implications of this are quite atrocious from any principled perspective. In order to have freedom, people must be forced, under threat of punishment by the State, to perform specific actions, or so Mr. Ellis would have us believe. This kind of tyrannical thinking is what brought us public school attendance, jury duty, the draft, and paying taxes. It is a bold mockery of the consent of the governed.

If you choose to vote, you CAN'T complain, since by voting you are already agreeing to the election results ahead of time; this is philosophical similar to when a court arbitrates a case, in that you are agreeing to the verdict ahead of time by being involved in a trial in the first place. I prefer to not participate or otherwise sanction the begging and groveling for smaller portions of wealth that were stolen at gunpoint. It is both a matter of honesty and pride to not pretend that dangerous illusions are beneficial to human beings, when the fact of the matter is, is that they are detrimental to the human experience in every conceivable way.

The American voting system has cheated, been broken, and lost the faith of considerable portions of the population, seeing that the least active mainline political process method is that of voting. Organizations such as Rock the Vote, MoveOn.org, Ron Paul's 2012 presidential campaign, and such others who have made it a point to encourage previously non-voting (or at least apolitical) people to vote are disingenuous for attempting to instill false hope in our struggle for Liberty. The consistent trend of decreasing voter turnout is a positive change and it should continue with paralleling increases of non-compliance with the Establishment as a whole.

For those who can't bear to not vote, the next best thing is to become a straight-ticket voter for the Libertarian Party. As much as their condescending attitude at LP chapter meetings towards newcomers and overall partyarchy irk me, they are the biggest third-party in America, being larger than all the other fringe parties put together. Another option is to go ahead and vote, but when you're in the booth, vote for the write-in candidate. You can write in a fictional character, yourself, a fellow dissident or hapless bystander that got railroaded by the government, or "None of the Above," (this is essentially a vote of no confidence). Hopefully by doing this, people will understand that the entire exercise is pure pabulum, and they will eventually regroup by exploring other methods that have a realistic chance for securing our Liberty.

Protesting Does Not Work

[April 16th, 2013]

A number of political dissidents consider human action to be purposeful behavior, but is it purposeful to do the same thing over and over again, and yet expect a different result? Would it not make more sense to question, in good faith, the viability of certain methods? Perhaps it would behoove us to seriously reevaluate given assumptions about some techniques of political activism.

Having paid attention to media coverage of street demonstrations over the past decade, it would seem that there are fundamentally three different kinds, or goals, of street protesting. The first is little more than being a grandstanding media whore, whereby grabbing the attention of the mainstream media "spreads awareness" about a particular topic, and that by itself, it is somehow going to mystically solve the problem of whatever the protester is bellyaching over. A variation on this is the street demonstrator who deliberately commits an act of civil disobedience in a blatantly public fashion (this is done so as to increase the probability they will be arrested by the police); the goal here is to rely on jury nullification in order to either set or reverse a judicial precedent, which will mystically somehow redress some other unrelated grievances. Finally, demonstrations provide a unique opportunity for dissidents to engage in a morale-raising spectacle with others who think like they do, all the while accomplishing little else.

The problem with each of these kinds of street protesters is that each variation not only regularly fails in achieving its ostensible aims, but also the fact that there exist better ways to achieve whatever it is they want. There are several mechanisms accessible to us that can be used in lieu of these ineffective types of protesting, sans the cost of police brutality (including, but certainly not limited to, baton charges and kettling) while simultaneously performing at least as well, if not dramatically better than, even the very best that such street demonstrations could have accomplished idyllically.

For instance, creating alternative media and culture jamming the Establishment's propaganda apparatus (through such methods such as subvertising, pranks, and especially meme hacks) appeals to both the mind and emotions of the public, instead of simply annoying the living fuck out of them. Ostracism of government informants, agent provocateurs, and deep-cover intelligence operatives is time well spent, instead of wasting it on constructing banners and flags that get rarely used on protest marches anyway. Discrete civil disobedience allows you to live free despite the arbitrary mala prohibita commanding dictates of the State. Informally small get-togethers at individual private homes is just as morale-raising as uselessly chanting, "Whose streets? Our streets!" or "This is what democracy looks like!" repeatedly in a public park like a bunch of mindless zombies. I would rather dissidents attend their local freedom festivals rather than waste their time, and risk what relatively little freedom they had left, by demonstrating in the street.

I still chuckle whenever one of my detractors claims that I'm acting inconsistent with my principles for publicly denouncing the viability of street demonstrations, as I've done in the past. The basic assertion is that I'm indescribably wicked or just simply mistaken for never even attending a protest. As I've said before, I have no intention of attending a protest of any kind, about anything, whatsoever. There is absolutely nothing about my political philosophy that requires me to act like a clueless hooligan. It would appear to be the case that the sycophantic followers of talk radio con-artists are pushing guilt trips if you don't succumb to their emotional rhetoric about your "failure" to participate in useless demonstrations.

Some dissidents consider street protests as a way of "fighting the system." This is fallacious, for they are not actually struggling, but whining about what ails the body politic. Simply complaining about Leviathan does not stop it; the withdrawal of consent (or as Ayn Rand put it, removing "the sanction of the victim"), coupled with defensive force, is what actually stops the march of statism. A sign waving coward is not a warrior for his people.

That's probably the worst part of protesting, the fact that it's nothing more than a proxy for real action. Instead of standing up and bravely disagreeing with the tyranny our people are suffering under, they elect to instead march through the streets as an amorphous mob, chanting manufactured slogans and waving cardboard protest signs. What cowardliness is this? They're treating it as if it were a compromise between the need to do something authentic and the fear of taking meaningful action that could actually accomplish something

According to Robert-Arthur: Menard, protesting is a type of acceptance giving legal permission to the government to do whatever it was they wanted to do in the first place. He suggested, in good faith, that what demonstrators ostensibly want to do is a public rejection of the regime's policies. Menard is fundamentally correct in that there are better ways of achieving the goals of activists rather than through street actions, such as by writing letters to bureaucrats or filing legal documents in court; of course, I doubt Menard understands the motivation behind the Carnival of Distractions, but his overall point is well taken, despite the fact that genuine sincerity is the exception, not the rule, of contemporary political activism.

Speaking of the disingenuous Patriot Rockstars who guilt trip their listeners, that reminds me of this much touted concept of "peaceful protesting" they've been pushing that I've heard about ad nauseum. Where the hell did this come from? Did everyone just forget about the Vietnam War protesters back in the 1960s who trail-blazed the technique of street demonstrating itself? Peaceful protesting seems little different from the dog training that TSA performs at airports nation wide; both are inherently designed to acclimate you into being docile and submissive to agents of the State who are the complete enemies of your liberty. Consider that Vietnam War protesters (including many of whom were returning veterans) understood that should the stormtrooper riot cops get rowdy, they still retained their natural liberty to defend themselves from such coercive violence with physical force.

Such an attitude is currently frowned on by these Patriot Rockstars who are badly attempting to emulate the so-called "civil rights leaders" of the past half century. One phony rhetorical trick says that self-defense might encourage agent provocateurs; this is, of course, the call sign of cowards, whelps, and pacifists. So-called "peaceful protesting" is intrinsically hypocritical, and demonstrates (pun intended) no commitment whatsoever to whatever principles they claim to hold. If there were any primary differences between the demonstrators of the '60s and those throughout the 2000s, it is that the latter don't think! Be very wary of those who advocate for "peaceful protesting," for they are the very same individuals who either do not have your best interest at heart, or are simply too naïve to understand what they are dealing with; either way, you are better off disregarding their useless advice.

A further distinction can be made about what the Vietnam War protesters did do. Demonstrations can work if they are performed for several years, by millions of people who are focused on a single objective (in this case, ending the Vietnam War), but activists now don't do that anymore because it's awfully passe to be actually focused on much of anything. It's sexy to be distracted by a myriad of problems rather than be seriously dedicated to a systemically pivotal goal. Who would want to actually solve problems when you can use the black bloc technique to bash in a window and steal an iPhone instead? It would seem to be the case that protesting now suffers from the broken window fallacy in much the same way the military-industrial complex does, as is manifested by the warfare–welfare State.

Sometimes, protests can possess the characteristics of a riot; however, what is to be gained by trashing a Starbuck's window? I am certainly no fan of corporatism, but acting out a temper tantrum like a spoiled brat is not going to bring the empty suit, fat cat CEOs to justice. Even worse, where is the justice in "keying" random cars, or throwing trash and scattering other undesirable debris around the place? Did none of these phony "anarchist" police snitches ever consider that just in terms of probability, they are much more likely to be damaging the property of some hapless nice folks rather than trashing the cars of the actual people responsible for what they claim to be upset about? Even if they are genuine non-propertarian anarchists, is it unreasonable for them to recognize that they are infringing upon the liberty of car owners by this form of intimidation? I have a sneaking suspicion that they just don't think!

Street actions could also work effectively if they are done in the form of rigidly organized rallies. This is what Marcus Garvey was doing with the UNIA back in the early 1920s. You want men who can mark perfectly in step, and who are dressed uniformly. That brings fear to the enemy. The closest this has come to actually happening was the 2012 Veterans for Ron Paul march, except for the fact they were individually dressed (we wouldn't want a repeat of Cpl. Jesse Thorton again, now would we?).

John Martinson has pointed out that there is such confusion about demonstrations being somehow revolutionary. As he has said:

"I suggest thinking of what it would be like to be the evil people in power. You look out your window and see a big sign. You chuckle inwardly, and then go back to plotting how you can profit from killing more people. Protests are not revolution. Holding signs and wearing T-shirts is not fighting. It's masturbation, it's whining, it's cowardly; it doesn't do anything.

"Signs are for armchair revolutionaries and weekend rebels. They can wave their sign, and although they know deep down that they haven't done anything, at all, they can be high and mighty to their Yuppie friends and say, 'I was there, man.' During the week, they look down on their co-workers and think, 'I'm actually trying to make a difference. I'm doing something, unlike the rest of you groveling wage-slaves.'

"Protests mattered when people were willing to pick up guns, or spears, or whatever the hell was close enough to them, to bludgeon the poor SOB who intended to take their life or liberty. Protests are also tactically inefficient, unless you intend to use mass chaos as a cover for another operation. A protest can be readily turned into a riot and the ease by which it can be has been proven by law enforcement agent provocateurs, time and time again. Then a ridiculous, futile, time-wasting crowd of thousands suddenly becomes their weapon; a tool for your oppression. They turn the protest into a riot, and that gives them more reason to clamp down; of course, the clamping down isn't the problem, it's the mindset. Authentic revolutionary action would mean a clamping down too, but in that case your men aren't sign waving cowards and weekend revolutionaries. They know what's coming, and they will respond with deadly force. So, there will be a clamping down on them, but they are prepared for that clamping down, because they are organized, because they're disciplined, because they're trained.

"When the mob transforms into a riot by the very people you intend to resist, they can only muster the courage to spray-paint buildings and throw bricks through windows. With the illusion of safety in numbers, they might even bruise a police officer, or take their aggression out on a fellow protester or passerby, as if that does anything."

I couldn't have said it better myself.

So, does protesting work? Not as it is practiced today, it doesn't. It utterly fails to secure anyone's Liberty. Worse yet, it is touted by the dissident opinion makers that if we don't do it, then you and I are somehow "negligent" in resisting tyrants. What a crock of shit they are, attempting to make use feel guilty for disagreeing with their fake "irrational exuberance." I say it's about damn time we took back the moral high ground from these change agents in sheep's clothing and demonstrate to them what true freedom really looks like by calling their bluff and offering alternatives to street protesting. Now might just be the time to spread the message of Liberty by teaching our own people what methodologically does not work by way of public ridicule, open scorn, and widespread contempt against those who seek to divert our energies from where they need to be allocated, if we are indeed going to be able to tackle the Establishment in any really effective way.

Grassroots Lobbying Does Not Work: A Review of Chris Cantwell's "Anarcho-Lobbyist" Series (Season One)

[June 29ᵗʰ, 2015]

Statists have always told libertarians that if we don't like the law, we should work to change it. Unfortunately, what this means is that if individuals want to secure their liberty, they must do so by begging for it from those tyrants who imagine themselves to be our rulers. Worse, some opportunists use this dynamic in order to put themselves on this week's news cycle, in order to further their own self-aggrandizement. As the Austrian economists put it, human action is purposeful behavior, yet, what behavior can be said to be purposeful if the actors are doing the same things over and over again, all the while expecting different results?

Grassroots political movements used to be all the rage in years past. During the 2008 banker bailouts, Americans witnessed the rise of the Tea Partiers, which the Ron Paul supporters originally began, but was then hijacked by disgruntled conservative fascists not long after. Following the 2011 Arab Spring, freegans and Greenbackers organized street demonstrations on Wall Street in New York City, yet, these too were quickly co-opted by disenchanted progressive communists.

Both the Tea Partiers and Occupiers of Wall Street ultimately issued demands for the government to act on their behalf in some way. Whether by petitioning or writing "their" congresscritters, the Tea Partiers and Occupiers attempted to redress their grievances by way of government, that is, through the political means of making money. If our enemy really is the State, then why do these political activists seek to curry favor with despots?

I suspect it is because they aspired to become the newest "special interests" by seeking reform, not abolition, of the State. Notice, for instance, the antipathy expressed by the Tea Partiers against cannabis, or the Occupiers against firearms. Worse yet, the response by most American patriots and libertarians to this controlled opposition is to support grassroots lobbying organizations, whether it be ones like Gun Owners of America (GOA) or the National Organization for the Reform of Marijuana Laws (NORML), in order to shrink the power of government.

A related underlying presumption here seems to be that if a man is opposed to the nationally organized grassroots lobbyists who want privileges bestowed upon them by the federal government, then he should refocus himself towards more "local" government, such as the municipality, county, or even provincial…*ahem*…"state" government he happens to be subject to the jurisdiction thereof. Some of the Free Staters in New Hampshire have "watch-dogged" the governments in Keene, Cheshire County, and Concord, and upon discovering the activities of the politicians, they started begging their local rulers to please be nicer to the body politic, as the New Hampshire Liberty Alliance (NHLA) has done.

Let me draw a rather significant distinction here regarding watch-dogging and grassroots lobbying. Merely attending public meetings and bearing witness to the daily routine of the State (as Shane Radliff has done recently with both the legislative and judicial branches of the McLean County government in Illinois), if done with the sincere intention of directly experiencing only what the State actually does, rather than believing through blind faith the incoherent civics nonsense spewed by the government propagandists known as "public school teachers," fails to compromise one's integrity in the cause for liberty. Grassroots lobbyists, I think, aspire to eventually infiltrate the State in order to turn it against itself; if such an absurd idea were to be taken seriously at all, it should first be experimented with, as Stefan Molyneux suggested, by infiltrating the Mafia with the explicit goal of turning it into the United Way.

Six months ago, in January of 2015, Christopher Cantwell began a new video series uniquely entitled, "Anarcho–Lobbyist," which is a tongue-in-cheek reference to the various flavors of hyphenated anarchism. In each episode, Cantwell usually approaches a desk, sits down, and then proceeds to tell a New Hampshire legislative committee exactly what he thought about whatever bill was being considered by them, including whether he supported it or not. Obviously, as you might be able to guess, I enjoyed his antics for its comedic value, to say nothing of the fairly cogent arguments underpinning his coy use of language.

Once I began evaluating his influence upon legislators, I noticed that I had also been subtly making unfounded assumptions regarding his motivations. Leaving absolutely nothing to chance, I decided to remove all supposition by calling in to the April 27th live stream of Cantwell's rebranded podcast, Radical Agenda, which is about "common sense extremism," as he describes it. During this third episode, I specifically asked him as to what his intentions where behind his pilgrimages to Concord [any mistakes in transcription are solely the fault of this humble blogger]:

Kyle Rearden: I was curious about your Anarcho-Lobbyist series. When you started it, and the subsequent videos that have rounded it out, were you attempting to influence legislators, or were you more just trying to kinda empirically demonstrate that grassroots lobbying does not work?

Chris Cantwell: Well, I suppose there's a couple of angles here, right? I take a certain amount of pleasure in going there and ranting before the legislature, some people seem to take an interest in it, I get to comment on policy, and whatnot. I do believe that some of these people have taken a great deal of interest in what I've said. I have yet to see if it actually tends to influence policy. I'd like it to influence policy, whenever I go in there and I say, "Hey, I shouldn't have to have a permit to carry a gun." I really do, I sincerely hope, that these guys say, "Hey, he's right, and we'll repeal that," and I hope that that happens, but if it turns out that these bills are getting defeated and that sort of thing, then we can see that it does not work. So, I'm going in there and doing it, and waiting to see what happens, more or less.

Think for a moment about the implications about what he just admitted. Cantwell, more or less, wants to have his cake and eat it too, quite possibly. On the one hand, he wants to "influence policy," which is reformism (that is, "working within the system in order to change it from within"), yet on the other hand, he appears comfortable in, say, taking one for the team, by demonstrating on video that grassroots lobbying these politicians does not work if the goal is to secure individual liberty. Although I can certainly appreciate his wait-and-see attitude, I find this to be an expression of wishful thinking, in that he seems to me to be presuming that if he is (marginally) successful in influencing legislators to shrink the power of government, then grassroots lobbying would not only become a technique worth doing, but also one worth being emulated by other libertarians outside of New Hampshire.

Earlier this month on June 5th, I called again, this time onto the fourteenth broadcast of Radical Agenda, in specific preparation for this article:

Kyle Rearden: Howdy Chris!, I wanted to first ask you if you had intended to make any more of those Anarcho-Lobbyist videos?

Chris Cantwell: I certainly do intend to, and as a matter of fact, I've got some good news on that front. That series was sort of dependent on…for awhile, I had a couple of problems with my vehicle. I knew I could fix them myself, but during the wintertime here, it was just too cold out for me to work on my car, so I back-burnered it, and I was uninspected and stuff, so to go to the capitol city of New Hampshire with my uninspected vehicle was sort of something prohibited and I was reliant on other people for that. I just today managed to get all the problems with my vehicle fixed, and I got my vehicle inspected, so I'll keep an eye on the House calendar, and when interesting things come up, I will be going up there, whether people want to come with me, or not.

Kyle Rearden: Well, part of the reason I wanted to ask you about that, Chris, was because I'm a blogger, and I had an article idea about writing a review of your Anarcho-Lobbyist series, but I did not want to write an article about something that is still going to have more episodes upcoming, so if you're going to have more episodes, I guess I could hold off on that, for the time being.

Chris Cantwell: Well, if you feel you have commentary on something that is already out there, you are certainly welcome to write any commentary you see fit, but I do intend to go back up to Concord. There's a certain period of time, and I don't entirely understand it myself, like, when I was doing them every week, there was a certain period of time when there was more of these things going on. When all the bills are first getting introduced, and the most interesting stuff is on the front burner, and that period has now passed, so some of the stuff that's going on is not necessarily as interesting. Some of the stuff I testified on is now being voted on in the House and Senate, and I don't really just wanna sit on the House floor and listen to these idiots argue with each other. There's not going to be as much of it, certainly, but there's still committee hearings and that sort of thing. I will be going up there, and you will see more Anarcho-Lobbyist, and when it comes back around next year, or more accurately, when that period comes this year, I might say more accurately (oh, well, I was doing them this year, or was it last year?)…anyway, when it comes around again, then I'll certainly have them out rapid fire, but it's gonna be a little slower. I'll be there in any case until that time.

Kyle Rearden: So, maybe, Chris, should I call it, "Season One" of Anarcho-Lobbyist versus "Season Two" in a sense, kinda like a television series, then?

Chris Cantwell: That wouldn't be a terribly inaccurate way to put it [inaudible] "holiday special," that kind of thing? We definitely had the most rapid fire period of it, it was during this period of time when all the most interesting bills are being testified on, so that would be sorta like season one and season two will be another set of rapid fire issues where we'll be going in there and talking about a lot of important things very quickly. I'm gonna be keeping an eye on the House and Senate calendars. If there are things that are worth going up there and talking about, now I'm at a point where I don't have to rely on anybody else. I can just go shoot up there and go whenever I want. We'll be back.

Notice that he announced here his intentions to make more installments of the Anarcho-Lobbyist series in the near future. Not only that, but he also acknowledged that the ones he's made up until now could be thought of as a collection unto themselves, hence my referencing of them as "Season One." In other words, the parameters of my review of his series are limited to this already released collection.

Briefly put, correlation does not imply causation. Just because there is no way to prove, from the available data sets, that Cantwell's lobbying caused the legislators to vote on the bills the way he wanted them to (because had their decisions been more in line with what he wanted, it still could just as easily have been due to coincidence), what my review can determine is whether Cantwell's lobbying is correlated to legislative decision-making.

Season One of the Anarcho-Lobbyist series was uploaded between January 30th to April 8th, encompassing 23 videos about 22 legislative bills, simply because HB 407 was the featured bill for both the February 11th and March 26th videos. A table of contents for Season One is as follows [dates follow a yy/mm/dd format]:

* 150130: Anarcho-Lobbyist vs. Bitcoin Regulators
* 150131: Anarcho-Lobbyist vs. E-Verify
* 150131: Anarcho-Lobbyist vs. Vehicle Inspections
* 150205: Anarcho-Lobbyist vs. Campaign Finance Reform
* 150205: Anarcho-Lobbyist vs. Stricter Voter Registration
* 150205: Anarcho-Lobbyist vs. Voter Registration Sharing
* 150205: Anarcho-Lobbyist vs. Absentee Ballots
* 150205: Anarcho-Lobbyist on Ballot Access
* 150205: Anarcho-Lobbyist vs. Open Primaries
* 150211: Anarcho-Lobbyist vs. Minimum Wage
* 150211: Anarcho-Lobbyist vs. Police Militarization
* 150213: Anarcho-Lobbyist for Constitutional Convention
* 150213: Anarcho-Lobbyist vs. State Lobbyists
* 150213: Anarcho-Lobbyist vs. Poker Regulators
* 150218: Anarcho-Lobbyist vs. Drug Prohibition
* 150219: Anarcho-Lobbyist for Bitcoin in Payment of Taxes
* 150221: Anarcho-Lobbyist vs. Civil Asset Forfeiture

❖ 150223: Anarcho-Lobbyist for Repealing Texting While Driving Ban
❖ 150224: Anarcho-Lobbyist for Jury Nullification
❖ 150325: Anarcho-Lobbyist for Constitutional Carry
❖ 150326: Anarcho-Lobbyist vs. Police Militarization, Round 2
❖ 150327: Anarcho-Lobbyist for an Article V Convention
❖ 150408: Anarcho-Lobbyist vs. Casino Corporatism

As you can no doubt tell, the political subject matter varied quite a bit, making it at least halfway decent for the variability of the overall data set. Listed here, in chronological order, are the corresponding bills to each of the videos (HB 407 is listed only once):

❖ HB 356: Bitcoin Regulators
❖ HB 267: E-Verify
❖ HB 387: Vehicle Inspections
❖ HB 649: Campaign Finance
❖ HB 627: Stricter Voter Registration
❖ HB 620: Voter Registration Sharing
❖ HB 659: Absentee Ballot
❖ HB 665: Ballot Access
❖ HB 652: Open Primary
❖ HB 370: Minimum Wage
❖ HB 407: Police Militarization
❖ HCR 1: Constitutional Convention
❖ HB 300: State Lobbyists
❖ HB 445: Poker Regulators
❖ HB 618: Drug Prohibition
❖ HB 552: Bitcoin in Payment of Taxes
❖ HB 475: Civil Asset Forfeiture
❖ HB 426: Repeal "Texting While Driving" Ban
❖ HB 470: Jury Nullification
❖ SB 116: Constitutional Carry
❖ HB 148: Article V Convention
❖ SB 113: Casino Corporatism

In terms of my research design, measuring Cantwell's effectiveness at influencing legislators can be easily determined by matching his support or opposition to a bill relative to whether the bill in question survived the legislative process at all, and if it did, discovering its current status. Put another way, Cantwell's advocacy in his videos can be measured against what the legislative committees eventually decided to do about the bills before them.

The results were quite revealing, to say the least. From the overall sample size of 22 bills, Cantwell's lobbying can be summarized thusly:

- ❖ For (n = 14)
    - o   HB 356: Retained in committee [lose]
    - o   HB 387: Inexpedient to legislate [lose]
    - o   HB 665: Inexpedient to legislate [lose]
    - o   HB 652: Inexpedient to legislate [lose]
    - o   HB 407: Ought to pass [win]
    - o   HB 300: Inexpedient to legislate [lose]
    - o   HB 445: Inexpedient to legislate [lose]
    - o   HB 618: Inexpedient to legislate [lose]
    - o   HB 552: Retained in committee [lose]
    - o   HB 475: Retained in committee [lose]
    - o   HB 426: Inexpedient to legislate [lose]
    - o   HB 470: Inexpedient to legislate [lose]
    - o   SB 116: Ought to pass [win]
    - o   HB 148: Enrolled [win]
- ❖ Against (n = 8)
    - o   HB 267: Inexpedient to legislate [win]
    - o   HB 649: Inexpedient to legislate [win]
    - o   HB 627: Inexpedient to legislate [win]
    - o   HB 620: Inexpedient to legislate [win]
    - o   HB 659: Retained in committee [win]
    - o   HB 370: Inexpedient to legislate [win]
    - o   HCR 1: Inexpedient to legislate [win]
    - o   SB 113: Inexpedient to legislate [win]

Assuming that "inexpedient to legislate" and "retained in committee" mean that the bills died in committee, then initial analysis reveals that only 3 of the 22 bills survived being in committee; in other words, 19 bills died in committee. Cantwell advocated for the passage of 14 bills, and opposed 8 other bills. All 8 of those bills died in committee, yet 11 bills Cantwell favored died as well, which means that those 3 bills that survived the committees were all supported by Cantwell; even then, only 1 has been scheduled for a floor debate.

In terms of success ratios, this means that Cantwell was batting 1:1 (100%) against those bills he opposed, yet only 3:14 (21%) in favor of those bills he supported. Averaging them out amongst the entire 22 bill sample, what this means is that Chris Cantwell's success ratio, overall, for the entirety of Season One, was 1:2 (50%). What this means is that a correlation between Cantwell's grassroots lobbying and the fate of a bill is not observable, because the probability is literally that of a coin toss, that is, random chance. In other words, there is no observable effect grassroots lobbying had on New Hampshire's legislative process at all within these measured samples.

Hitchens' razor says that the burden of proof lies only with the claim maker; skeptics are not required to provide evidence disproving the claims in question in order to be correct. Yet, in the interests of furthering everyone's remedial political education, I have found it both illustrative and necessary to go above and beyond the call of duty, as it were, and explore whatever proof is available, especially including that which debunks reformism. In this critique of grassroots lobbying, my only interest lies in discovering the truth of such lobbying's effectiveness in shrinking or abolishing whatever elements of government that are realistically possible.

Not only has causation not been proved by reformists, but in fact, the Anarcho-Lobbyist's first season appears to suggest that even correlation is irrelevant. This likely means that legislative advocacy organizations, such as the NHLA, are at best, irrelevant to mainstream political decision-making. In light of this revelation, I wouldn't be surprised if such a result were eventually proved to also be accurate here in Texas, simply because the legislature here in Austin is less accessible than the one in Concord, in part due to the fact that Texan legislators don't allow open carry at their capitol building, unlike in Concord where Cantwell demonstratively proved open carry as being tolerable to the New Hampshirite legislators inside their own capitol building without undue incident from the government police.

My working hypothesis, as implied by the title of this article, is that grassroots lobbying does not work, simply because legislators seek to always increase the power of government. The only real problem with this hypothesis, even if objectively true, is that it assumes a causation that cannot be measured from the already presented data set. All that this data can show, at most, is whether or not a correlation existed between Cantwell's lobbying and legislative committee actions. As already demonstrated, there is not any observable correlation between these two variables, since Cantwell's overall success ratio is literally that of a coin toss.

In light of this truth, Cantwell might as well have stayed home and the probability would have remained exactly the same; however, this does beg the question as to the value of the work he put into Season One of the Anarcho-Lobbyist series. Although Cantwell incurred opportunity costs, what he was able to accomplish was bringing transparency to the very act of grassroots lobbying itself through both his articles and videos, thereby surpassing the NHLA by leaps and bounds in this regard. Without Cantwell's efforts at transparency, I wouldn't have been able to review his attempts at lobbying, and judge its efficacy accordingly; for that alone, I thank him quite profusely.

Truth be told, using the scientific method does entail the repeatability of experiments, so should anyone else, especially those who is believe in reformism, be interested in mimicking Cantwell's Anarcho-Lobbyist series, preferably with a larger sample size and a more consistent bibliography than he kept, I'd certainly encourage them to do so. My hope is that how I collected and analyzed the data here provides a good example in how to gather such evidence for a data set, and especially the importance of follow-up once the legislature has had enough time to make its decisions, especially regarding committee actions.

Long-term strategic and methodological considerations need better efficacy than that of random chance if anyone is serious about securing their liberties. Once the wheat has been separated from the chaff, and the latter thrown into the dustbin of failed political action, then perhaps Americans will be more willing to examine the wheat that is left and see what it has to offer. Whether such wheat has a reliable historical track record, or is just experimental, such a class of tactics should be given serious consideration, rather than just dismissively ignored in favor of the chaff that promises nothing but repeated failures. If indeed Ludwig von Mises was correct that human action is purposeful behavior, then the best way, as I see it, of honoring his legacy is to debunk reformism and its failed techniques for the counterproductive distraction that it is.

At this juncture, given what I've just shown about grassroots lobbying, it is probably accurate to say that anyone who recommends libertarians to speak in front of any legislative body, with the intention of trying to persuade the legislators to please be nicer to the population-at-large, is someone who is very naïve about the nature of the situation we are all suffering under, which is, namely, statism. Consider William Wolf's unsuccessful attempt, back in February of 2014, at requesting the Gallatin County Commissioners to form a three-member panel in order to investigate government corruption in Montana. Although one could argue that this was an isolated case, consider also the advocacy by some to use any opportunity to speak in front of a legislative body as their own personal bully pulpit.

Rather than beleaguer the sopping wet pathetic failure that reformism is any further, I would like to briefly suggest a few alternatives to grassroots lobbying. Escaping the State through such legal remedies as cancelling your voter registration (or quite possibly, expatriation), is far more effective than begging the rulers for scraps from the King's table. Sam Konkin's agorist philosophy and counter-economic methods promise a way for people to civilly disobey the rulers while side-stepping the alleged necessity for legal defense fund scams (for the most part).

Arguably, if libertarian vigilantes were able to retain both their guns and privacy, then they would possess the means to win all their other freedoms back, not unlike the Polish resistance of last century.

Lobbying, whether grassroots or otherwise, is not "fighting." Much like protesting, it's a form of begging, albeit, more dignified begging. I don't know about the rest of you all, but as for me, I'd rather exercise my own natural liberty without asking permission, rather than wasting a single moment of my valuable time in the physical presence of those delusional predators by groveling before them like a sniveling coward.

[Postscript: I'd like to acknowledge and thank Shane Radliff for his help in tracking down the remainder of the legislative bills so I could discover what their current status was, for without that knowledge, this article would not have been possible in fairly judging the efficacy of the Anarcho-Lobbyist series thus far.]

Running for Public Office Does Not Work: Why "Infiltrating the State" is Foolish

[July 9th, 2015]

People feel indescribably trapped by this horrendous system that grinds us down, and it does so primarily by its very irrationality. Despite all the rhetoric you may hear about the practicality of elections, this is little else than badly constructed sophistry whose purpose is to suck American dissidents right back into the coercive government structure by increasing their opportunity costs. Failure to objectively judge the dangers inherent within the political means of making money reinforces the hapless citizenry's Stockholm Syndrome with the State.

All anyone has to do, in order to determine the efficacy of trying to "infiltrate the State" with the explicit goal of either shrinking or abolishing it, is to discover how many elections have been won and how many laws have been repealed by those who claim to value individual liberty. Remember, all Hitchens' razor demands is that the claim maker substantiate their claims with evidence; it is not incumbent on any critics, logically, to provide evidence debunking the claims in question (which would be attempting to prove a negative). Unfortunately for those who advocate running for public office as a viable technique for securing liberty, I have seen no evidence supporting their baseless assertions.

History is valuable because it reminds the future about the mistakes of the past, in the hope that they can learn a lesson or two from them. The 2004 "Libertarian" Party (LP) presidential debate between Gary Nolan, Michael Badnarick (the author of Good to be King), and Aaron Russo, while certainly entertaining, did not result in any electoral wins. Despite having ballot access in 49 of the several states, Badnarick, as the LP's presidential nominee, still failed to win the U.S. Presidency, ultimately receiving 0.32% of the popular vote, and more importantly, none from the Electoral College (whose votes are required by the 1787 federal Constitution for the presidency).

Christopher Cantwell ran against Tim Bishop for his seat in the House of Representatives for New York's first congressional district, back in 2010. Cantwell was joined by his campaign manager, Gary Donoyan, for an interview with Joseph Dobrian for the December 10th, 2009 broadcast of Hardfire, which is the only time I've ever seen Cantwell wear a suit and tie. His first venture into standup comedy took place at the LibertyFest NYC on September 10th of 2011, where he was introduced as a former aspiring politician; needless to say, Cantwell failed to beat Bishop.

Ron Paul ran three presidential campaigns, first in 1988, then 2008, and finally in 2012. As the LP nominee in '88, Dr. Paul had ballot access in 46 of the several states and he received 0.47% of the popular vote; twenty years later in '08, Dr. Paul failed to gain the GOP nomination, mainly because he only managed to get 1 – 2% of the delegates to pledge to him, and due to the shenanigans of the GOP at Tampa three years ago, Dr. Paul only got 8.31% of the vote for the party's nomination. The receipts for these campaigns came out thusly:

- ❖ 1988: $2,000,000
- ❖ 2008: $28,100,000
- ❖ 2012: $40,947,039

Despite both the financial and opportunity costs incurred by Ron Paul's supporters, academics like Walter Block stubbornly insist on the political means of making money as being somehow viable to the cause of liberty. As Dr. Block said on The Lew Rockwell Show, episode 296, broadcasted on July 27th of 2012:

"How do we expect to win? The only way we can expect to win and bring about a libertarian society is to have a lot of libertarians. And how do you get a lot of libertarians? Well, the vehicle of the political process. I think Ron Paul has empirically demonstrated this, so, I don't want to jettison the political process because we can use it as a means, as a vehicle, as Ron Paul has shown, to promote liberty, even though the thing itself is rotten to the core, as you [Lew Rockwell] point out."

If Dr. Block means that running for public office is useful as a vehicle for raising campaign contributions, then I most certainly agree with him on that one, for as Penny Freemen told Adam Kokesh a month earlier, Dr. Paul's portfolio has definitely grown, because of his presidential campaigns. Interestingly enough, Dr. Paul himself had something to say about the efficacy of his time in public office during his farewell address to Congress:

"In many ways, according to conventional wisdom, my off-and-on career in Congress, from 1976 to 2012, accomplished very little. No named legislation, no named federal buildings or highways — thank goodness. In spite of my efforts, the government has grown exponentially, taxes remain excessive, and the prolific increase of incomprehensible regulations continues. Wars are constant and pursued without Congressional declaration, deficits rise to the sky, poverty is rampant and dependency on the federal government is now worse than any time in our history… I have come to one firm conviction after these many years of trying to figure out 'the plain truth of things.' The best chance for achieving peace and prosperity, for the maximum number of people world-wide, is to pursue the cause of LIBERTY." [emphasis added]

Right there, Dr. Paul is directly contradicting what Dr. Block had said just four months earlier. How can infiltrating the State by winning elections and repealing laws be effective in securing liberty if your top champion explicitly stated just how much of a failure he was doing just that over the course of 36 years?

Some people have asserted, time and again, that it doesn't matter whether running for office actually works to promote the cause of liberty, because it's their "right" to run such campaigns in the first place. Constitutionally speaking, the federal one is silent on this, although it does mention the eligibility for the presidency in Art. II § 1 cl. 5, as well as for representatives and senators in Art. I § 2 cl. 2 & Art. I § 3 cl. 3, respectively; therefore, the 10th Amendment takes effect. Similarly, the 1876 Texas Constitution appears equally silent on the alleged "right" to run for office, at most stating which public offices are constitutionally established, and at times mentioning the length a citizen may hold such offices. Honestly, the only constitution I am aware of that enumerates a "right" to run for office is, quite literally, the 1972 Socialist Constitution of the Democratic People's Republic of Korea. Article 66 says:

"All citizens who have reached the age of 17 have the right to elect and to be elected, irrespective of sex, race, occupation, length of residence, property status, education, party affiliation, political views or religion. Citizens serving in the armed forces also have the right to elect and to be elected. A person who has been disenfranchised by a Court decision and a person legally certified insane do not have the right to elect or to be elected."

If that sounds good to you, you might want to first watch PBS' Frontline broadcast on January 14th of 2014 in order to gain some perspective.

Given that running for public office might as well be just another government program, then what are the rules imposed by the State? Limiting ourselves to only Texas provides a wealth of information, courtesy of both the Texas Secretary of State's Qualifications for Office webpage and the Texas Election Code, which I will overview briefly now. Texas Election Code § 141.001 says that a candidate must be a United

States citizen, 18 years old or older, have resided in Texas for a year, to not have been legally determined to be either partially or totally mentally incapacitated, and to satisfy any other eligibility requirements prescribed by law for the office being sought.

But wait, there's more! Election Code § 141.031 says that the candidate must apply for a place on the ballot, essentially making what appears to be an affidavit, and § 141.035 says that the application and "an accompanying petition" is public information immediately upon filing. Independent (that is, nonpartisan) candidates are required by § 142.002 to make a declaration of intent to run, § 142.004 says that in addition to the application from § 141.031, an independent candidate must also file a petition to satisfy § 141.062.

Probably the simplest location for discovering what is required of candidates is to look at the Independent Candidates and Write-In Candidates webpages, courtesy of the Texas Secretary of State. If you are running as an independent candidate for a district, county or precinct office, then for your petition you must collect 500 signatures or 5% of the total vote, whichever is lesser, pursuant to § 142.007. For write-in candidates, they must collect a somewhat similar proportion of signatures, unless they prefer to pay a filing fee in lieu of getting signatures, which could range anywhere from $375 – $3,750, depending upon office being sought and population of a given electorate, pursuant to §§ 146.023(b), 146.0232, & 172.025; of course, this is different for a candidate in a primary where the filing fee ranges from $300 – $1,500 depending on the office, pursuant to § 172.024.

American patriots, I suspect, are not going to seriously plow through all the legal jargon in order to understand how to get their militiamen elected as county sheriffs just in time for the 2016 elections next year. All that the Texas Constitution has to say about county sheriffs is that they are elected every 4 years (Art. V § 23), they double as tax collectors in counties under a population of 10,000 (Art. XVI § 61), they receive free medical services paid for by the Texas government (Art. III § 52e), and, like all other elected and appointed officials, sheriffs take an oath not only to the Texas Constitution, but also the federal one as well (Art. XVI § 1).

I guess that explains why the Texas government left KC Massey to rot in solitary, despite the conflict of laws. So much for "oath-keeping" and "constitutional sheriffs," especially considering the fake drone attack retreat during last year's Bundy Affair, despite the ridiculous excuses offered later. To paraphrase Matthew 6:24, you can't serve two masters, but that didn't bother the speakers none at the Come & Take It! rally in San Antonio, back on October 19th of 2013.

Should you feel baffled, at this point, as to the sheer irrational complexity of running for public office, you are certainly not alone. Naomi

Wolf mentioned in her book, Give Me Liberty, about how her socially democratic populist expectations were just crushed by the sheer weight of bureaucracy:

> "I had told the young woman in Wisconsin to run for city council. Now I needed to see if I knew how to run myself and if I could help other people run. But I found that not only was usable information about democracy disappearing, so were the entry points to citizen leadership. I accumulated a stack of research materials from all the main resources a citizen would plausibly turn to if he or she wanted to run for office: state and city government, governors' offices, Congress, county sources, and so on. I kept having a bizarre intellectual experience… [t]here is no way to know how to get one of those seats for yourself if you are a citizen – no way to compete fairly with the donors, cronies, members of special interests, lovers, business colleagues, or other people filling the seats that an American citizen should have free and fair and equal access to."

She went on to complain that there are no idiot-proof tutorials about how to become an elected ruler. Ironically, she discovered how enlisting in the federal U.S. Army was amazingly user-friendly:

> "When I had knocked on the door to this avenue of my possible public service, I found that the entry point could not have been clearer, better guided, or better designed to help me through the process…[i]n parting, I received several gifts. I received a number of illustrated brochures… I received a free DVD… I also got a coffee mug."

Wolf presumes that democractic governments should go out of their way to lower the barriers to entry for citizens to directly contest the seats of incumbents. She fails to understand that this is exactly how the system is designed to work. Because the Stateis intrinsically a violently (anti-propertarian) coercive monopoly, it establishes barriers to entry in order to entrench those who imagine themselves to be our rulers upon their hallucinatory thrones. To paraphrase John Rockefeller, competition is sinful.

What are the contemporary attitudes of running for public office? Free Keene's Ian Bernard is very much in favor of other people running for local (that is, municipal or county) offices, such as when he praised Tim O'Flaherty's electoral win in Manchester's Ward 5 as an oxymoronic anarchist politician. By contrast, Liberate RVA, from what I can tell, has been staunchly against popular electoral voting, which implies seeking political office as well. In 2007, Stefan Molyneux argued why infiltrating the State is foolish:

> "Why don't you join the Mafia, and turn them around? Turn them into the United Way, turn them into a nice group, or at least, get them to give up significant portions of their business. Join the Mafia, get them to give up half their gambling control, half their control of the prostitution rings, get them to give up half of their shakedowns, and half of their drug trade. Or a third. Or 10%! You can do that, and you will learn enormously valuable lessons about how to actually go about changing an institution, which everybody still considers moral and which has a huge and massive army. [*chuckles*] Do you see why it looks a little funny, I mean seriously, do you see why it looks a little bit funny for people to say, as one guy did, 'Oh no, you see, Ron Paul, he's going to make the world better and safer by closing down all the army bases, ending the war in Iraq, and bringing the military home.' If you know how to control and minimize the biggest army the world has ever seen, then surely, infiltrating the Mafia and turning it around should be nothing to you. It should be a weekend's work."

Molyneux described earlier in his vlog that the ability to infiltrate any organization and then turn it completely against its own membership has not been demonstrated to be feasible by reformists. If the LP's aspiring politicians do not possess the ability to infiltrate the KKK and turn it into the NAACP, then why would anyone assume they can infiltrate the State in order to turn it against itself by abolishing, or at least, shrinking it? I think the empirical record, as well as Molyneux's cogent reasoning debunking this nonsense, should put to rest this silly advocacy that says dissidents should run for office.

Reformists who advocate for "liberty-minded candidates" to run for office willfully ignore electoral history, and they know even less about the law. If Fred Rodell was correct in saying that the law is a racket, then that slogan automatically debunks the viability of infiltrating the State by running for office by itself, simply because the only good reason for dissidents to become politicians is to repeal as many laws as humanly possible. If nobody showed up to vote, would there still be an election? If so, then the problem here is that those running for office are inherently relying on voter turnout in order to infiltrate the State.

Political processes don't matter in the final equation, despite the empty bleating from reformists like Naomi Wolf and Walter Block. What does matter is enforcement. If the legislature passed a bill into law, and the police don't enforce it, then what relevance does it have to your life in any real practical way?

In terms of "getting the message out," political parties and running for office are, in fact, terribly ineffective ways to go about do so. Much better alternatives are educational organizations, such as the International Society for Individual Liberty and the Foundation for Economic Education. Vloggers such as Stefan Molyneux and Eric English, both of whom started their respective channels in August of 2006, have gotten over 58 million and 5 million total videos views, respectively. Since reformists themselves frequently use the alternative media for their own publicity, all I'm asking for, from them, is to have a minimum degree of ends-means consistency, particularly in light of the fact that they are not totally adverse to the economic means of making money.

Truth be told, I wouldn't be surprised if the advocates of running for public office only did so because they honestly don't know what else to do that would be more effective in terms of securing their liberties. Maybe if they were to cultivate a sense of patience, they would begin to understand the wisdom inherent in role-playing police interrogations, celebrating freedom holidays, and reclaiming unclaimed property. Until such time they give up working within the system, reformists will simply spin around endlessly in circles with no solutions, no real options, and no foreseeable way off the carousel of carnivores.

Filming Government Agents Does Not Work

[November 29th, 2013]

Police officers have bullied Americans for far too long. Their incessantly rampant abuse of our liberty is absolutely intolerable; so, the question then becomes, what can Americans do to hold these disgusting cops accountable? Reformists tend to think that working within the judicial branch of government, as well as raising public awareness of this truly horrific epidemic, are viable approaches that should be taken to protect Americans, yet they have failed to address any critiques to their methodology that are offered in good faith.

For over the better part of a decade, it has become a frequent technique for American political dissidents to film government agents, albeit with different stylistic approaches. The first version is now known as "copblocking," which is defined as the act of filming police officers during an encounter of some kind (such as a traffic stop) with the goal of providing objective transparency for the event, especially if the situation were to degenerate violently. A variation on this are called "confrontations," whereby citizens initiate an encounter with a politician (usually either a legislator or a bureaucrat) with the goal of asking hardball questions in order to solicit a response they hope is demonstrative of governmental tyranny. Both approaches share the attributes of using digital consumer electronics (especially hand-held video cameras) and those videos of such encounters are made publicly available by being uploaded to an Internet video-sharing website, such as YouTube.

A commonly annoying habit of such government agents, but especially that of cops, is of claiming during such encounters that they would prefer to not be filmed, either because doing so would interfere with their investigation, or because it violates their individual privacy. Last time I checked, unless police investigations are confidential affairs performed under the auspices of secrecy, I don't understand why they would have a problem with the collection and storage of data. Although individual privacy is held as one of the most sacrosanct of personal liberties, the moment a person dons a uniform (or is otherwise representing the government in his official capacity), any reasonable expectation of privacy is forfeited so long as he operates as an agent of the State. There are tradeoffs to be considered whenever statists want to assume coercive power and forceful domination over their fellow man.

Filming government agents requires a savvy knowledge of consumer electronics. The main piece of equipment is a digital video camera, whether hand-held or strapped to one's body in some fashion. Prices of these consumer goods range from somewhat cheap to pretty expensive, typically $80 – $1,500. Most of these cameras rely on SanDisk (SD) memory cards, which range in price from $8 – $300, depending on quality and capacity; it should also be noted that there is an emerging trend towards live-streaming capability, primarily because some unfortunate copblockers have had police confiscate their SD cards. Despite the high technology currently available for sale, I can't help but wonder what the tradeoffs for dissidents would be regarding their wish for government transparency relative to the privacy implications of frequently using such surveillance equipment; put another way, does the utilization of the equipment required for filming government agents inadvertently acclimate dissidents towards regularly practicing sousveillance, and if so, would this be evidence of them tacitly supporting the justifications made for the existence of the surveillance police state apparatus?

As much as the technique of filming cops and politicians has been heralded by the alternative media as if it were indisputably wonderful, there has been little follow-up as to how effective such as method is for providing transparency and accountability in any level of government. Unfortunately, such "transparency" and "accountability" are vaguely defined, if at all, and their lack of applicability to filming government agents just comes across as nothing more than empty activist rhetoric. When you consider how such accountability is to be enforced, there are only two ways this could possibly be done with copblocking and confrontations, respectively – the number of cops being dragged into court and getting convicted, and the number of politicians who were fired or otherwise thrown out of office; in other words, how many cops have been punished and how many politicians have lost their jobs because of "copblocking" and "confrontations?"

Sadly, neither copblocking nor confrontations have conclusively demonstrated to have held police and politicians accountable for their tyrannical actions. Wishful thinking predominates the minds of activists, who are sincerely desperate for anything that might be able to prevent, mitigate, or expose the misdeeds of government. Despite this, are there two chief arguments offered by such filming advocates, one for reformism explicitly, and the other in favor of public awareness. I would like to offer four different rebuttals to these two arguments in the hope that these assertions can either be finally debunked, or at least greatly challenged.

The reformist argument claims that "we" should hold government agents accountable for their actions by documenting their atrocities for the benefit of the court, so they can be convicted and punished later. My utilitarian rebuttal is that there is no provable track record demonstrating the effectiveness of copblocking, other than the trend of documenting the existence of the abuse itself. If the police encounter leads to a hearing or even a trial, all that the prosecutor has to do is to file a motion for suppression of evidence regarding the recording in question, and if the judge grants that motion (or even arbitrarily declares the evidence as somehow inadmissible), then the defendant's case is greatly handicapped, if not outright lost, because in a strict contest between a citizen's testimony versus that of a police officer's "expert" testimony, the cop wins hands down (with regards to politicians, the underlying assumption is that some of them can be voted out of office, which is silly to assume because not only does it fail to address the bureaucracy, but it also neglects to mention the fact that voting does not work). My deontological rebuttal is that copblocking and confrontations both require direct physical contact with government agents, so unless you are only "working within the system" for some guerrilla purpose (such as whistle-blowing, paper-tripping, or monkey-wrenching), then you are engaging in reformist tactics (such as litigation); if you want nothing to do with the State, then filming government agents is contradictory to your own goals because it increases your direct contact with the government that much more than if you had not.

Advocates further assert that regardless of the reformist argument, video-taping cops and politicians is still valuable because of its propaganda value, so as to motivate people to become minarchists. My utilitarian rebuttal is that there is no proof demonstrating this to be true at all; in fact, there is already a plethora of police brutality videos on YouTube, as there are numerous confrontation videos. Although one could infer it might be effective in moving an individual along the other (not so) thin line, this is still wishful thinking (and for those who have had personal experience where they know for certain that these videos did help someone else to begin caring about their liberty, they certainly aren't talking about it publicly). My deontological rebuttal is that if uploading videos of abusive cops and corrupt politicians were valuable as propaganda, then the whole facade of trying to "hold them accountable" would be broken in the minds of the viewers because the footage would very strongly suggest that you cannot hold such government agents "accountable" at all. Considering also the historical precedent that much lesser forms of proof were sufficient for motivating vigilante justice against such government agents, as well as the fact that there is no trend of cops being frequently shot or politicians being regularly tarred and feathered before being run out of town on a rail, then this would mean (more likely than not) that such copblocking and confrontations utterly fail to motivate dissidents to do much of anything else other than run around and film these government agents some more; if anything, I would further suggest that such a profuse diet of unproductively volatile footage serves to promote fear and anger against the government without a guerrilla remedy or some other outlet for such frustration, thus this discontent is left to fester and eat away at your soul.

I find it ironic that anarchists spearheaded the development of this method. Perhaps their motivation lay in the assumed propaganda value of trying to delegitimize the State by recording the atrocities and abuses committed by government agents. Yet, with regards to reformism (and particularly to copblocking), I question their integrity simply because if they maintain that the State does not exist, then why does something that does not exist need to be held accountable at all? As Pete Eyre said:

"Having an objective record of the interaction between yourself or somebody else and police employees is crucial because if something goes down and you don't have that video, then it's a situation where it's you versus their word, and when their friends are the people judging the situation they tend to side with those folks with badges, so the camera creates that transparent record and speaks truth."

Maybe Eyre doesn't understand this communications medium all that well, but this just isn't always true. Anyone who has ever played around with videography knows how easy it is to manipulate and edit footage. An abuse of this ability to do so has been argued previously by Gary Hunt in his seminal article, *Because YouTube Said So...* (an audio version of the article is also available). Having been on that side of the fence not that long ago, I can more deeply appreciate than most so-called "activists" the inherent dangers of overly relying on film as a way to secure my liberties. Although I still enjoy watching open-source documentaries on "BoobTube," I am now much more discriminating when I analyze the claims being made, in much the same manner as I study mainstream television.

Another element of these confrontations and copblocking episodes is how the cameraman will constantly interrupt the government agent, and thus not allow him the opportunity to give him enough rope to hang himself with. This is very noticeable, particularly with the confrontations of politicians, and leaves the viewer either titillated with reality TV excitement, or amazingly frustrated. Take the style of James O'Keefe, for instance. Regardless of your attitude towards his undercover exposes of ACORN back in 2009, what was valuable about what O'Keefe did was how he was able to elicit a response from his interviewed subjects. Although his techniques might not work well during copblocking, it would certainly have increased the probability of success in getting any answer from politicians in those confrontation videos; in that sense, I think it is more than fair to say that James O'Keefe totally upstaged Luke

Rudkowski, and rightfully so (ironically, even though Rudkowski has made a name for himself in the alternative media for these so-called "confrontations," he himself behaves exactly like one of those politicians whenever anyone else tries to "confront" him about anything).

Unfortunately, copblocking and confrontations can become a danger to your financial health, if you let it. Far from encouraging you to frugally enjoy your liberty, the hobby of filming government agents has quickly become evocative of anti-free market corporate consumerism. For example, Rudkowski admitted that he has a $20 shoulder harness, a Go Pro camera ($200 – $400), a DSLR 60-D ($500 -$1,500), an iPhone ($50 – $700, depending on series and capacity), an Android cellular telephone ($100 – $200), a $5 adapter between the iPhone and the Android phone, and an Energizer XP18000 Universal AC Adapter with External Battery ($150). A year later, Eyre judged Rudkowski's updated equipment as being terrific, especially since Rudkowski added to his kit a custom wireless microphone, a pair of goggles, a walkie-talkie, video recording glasses ($50 – $150), police scanner with earpiece ($90 – $500), and multiple unrevealed hidden cameras. I guess Rudkowski had to figure out a way to spend all that donation money, and it would seem to be the case that he did, even if he had to engage in the odd activist legal defense fund scam to do it.

Once you understand that cops aren't even constitutional, then you begin to also understand why any notion of trying to "hold them accountable" by filming them seems rather ineffective. Considering also how the American prison population is by far the largest in the world in what is ironically called "the land of the free," how police at all levels of government actively encourage a snitch culture, and what you should contemplate doing to protect yourself from these insatiable predators, it becomes quite clear that any notion of "working within the system" is just pure lunacy. Filming cops will not save you from jail, and filming politicians will not stop them from passing whatever unconstitutional statutes they damn well want. The only possible exception to this rule would be if you recorded a police officer at a traffic stop using a digital audio recorder($30 – $80); however make sure ahead of time that either you live in a "one party" state (such as Texas), or in the case of a "two-party" state, make sure to get the officer's consent, otherwise the tape is worse than useless because you could be prosecuted if you were ever caught with that recording, or if it was made public. Besides this mitigation, the only realistic moves you have left is to strongly encourage these government agents to voluntarily quit their jobs while you discretely form security teams; never forget that the government jobs that comprise entire police departments and judicial courts are just another welfare state handout.

In conclusion, it saddens me to bear witness to how individuals have been suckered into counter-productive hobbies that unnecessarily increases their opportunity costs. This is by no means a "holier-than-thou" statement, for even the best of us get suckered in by the unmitigated promotion of bad techniques like this, for even Chris Cantwell goes cop blocking. Perhaps someday when more of us learn how to strategically plan, as well as how to objectively evaluate our tactics, then maybe Liberty can indeed be secured once again from the ravaging monsters who inhabit the darkest corners of the human soul.

Suing the Government Does Not Work: Lawsuits Are Not Useful For Securing Your Liberty

[July 14th, 2015]

Lawsuits are the judicial equivalent of ballots. If ballots are a substitute for bullets, then wouldn't that mean lawsuits are also a substitute for bullets? Reformists insist that if "we" Americans sue the government more often for their corrupt abuses of our common freedoms, then our liberty would become secured. I contend instead that reformists have not satisfied their burden of proof for demonstrating the efficacy of lawsuits in shrinking the power of the State.

Reformists incompletely praise any goal of lawsuits, because for them to do so would be to reveal some ugly truths about the nature of modern American democracy. Certainly, while it is true that lawsuits could (hypothetically) be used by patriots, libertarians, and other types of dissidents to hold the government (somewhat) accountable by constraining its power (somehow), revenge against "public sector" employees is also an equally probable reason for suing the government. Enrichment for the plaintiff's own wallet is an less frequently admitted motive, especially considering the damage such a "money-grubbing" image would cast upon the reputations of various litigants.

Hypothesizing about the efficacy of anything is not very useful if your a priori reasoning is less than convincing. This is largely why I prefer, when dealing with my opponents, to rely more heavily on whatever empiricism I can muster on behalf of human liberty. To that end, I will be examining a little over half a dozen lawsuits in order to determine, within the parameters of the sample, whether lawsuits are conducive to the restoration of our common freedom.

Judge Alice Batchelder ruled in the American Civil Liberties Union v. National Security Agency, Nos. 06-2095/2140 (2007) case that the plaintiffs lacked standing to challenge the NSA's Stellar Wind surveillance program because they couldn't prove they were directly targeted by it. In other words, the ACLU was unable to challenge the constitutionality of the wiretapping itself because, by its very nature, Stellar Wind was a dragnet. According to that line of judicial reasoning, then I suppose those mobile X-ray vans roaming neighborhood streets are just as equally "constitutional" in their warrantless searches, am I right?

Judge John Bates ruled in the Oberwetter v. Hilliard & Salazar, No. 09-0588 (2010) case that the plaintiff's lawsuit was dismissed because "expressive dancing" was a "public demonstration," and therefore it was categorically disruptive to the tranquil and contemplative mood enforced at the Jefferson Memorial by the National Park Service. This is not an attempt by the government at chilling free expression, to paraphrase the judge, since the government is being "viewpoint neutral" by prohibiting all demonstrations; apparently, it also turned out that the Jefferson Memorial is a "nonpublic forum," which is why "public demonstrations" are banned. Needless to say, this didn't stop Adam Kokesh from dancing at the Jefferson Memorial on both May 28thand June 4th of 2011.

Besides the property ownership issue, there is also an element here regarding the use of force, which is why I think this case uniquely angers philosophically consistent libertarians. Oberwetter was accosted by Hilliard who ripped out her earbud, violently twisted her arm, shoved her against a pillar, and subsequently arrested her for "disturbing the peace," releasing her 5 hours later. A few days later, Hilliard issued her two citations, one for "demonstrating without a permit," and another for "interfering with an agency function." Hilliard failed to properly prepare the matter for a court hearing and he neglected to proceed further in prosecuting Oberwetter.

Why is this significant? Judge Bates ruled that Hilliard cannot be sued by Oberwetter because Oberwetter did not have the right to "expressively dance" within a "nonpublic forum." Due to this, Hilliard did have probable cause to arrest Oberwetter, because she was violating the administrative regulation against demonstrating within a "nonpublic forum." Furthermore, Hilliard, as an officer, had the "authority" to use coercion during the course of an arrest in order to successfully effect it; since there was no observable injury to Oberwetter after the fact, Hilliard's use of force was, therefore, not excessive.

So, if a domestic abuser were to mimic the result of Hilliard's violence with a sack of oranges, considering Judge Louie Brandeis' warning in 1928 that the government teaches the whole people by its example, does that mean the battered spouse cannot seek financial recompense? Oh, wait, silly me…I assumed that the State existed within the ethical boundaries the rest of humanity commonly abides by. Yet, despite the spontaneous order of the free market, I tremble to contemplate that, without any government, who would violently slam dancing women against stone pillars?

Judge Sam Lindsay ordered that the Dobbs v. Farrell & Helleson, No. 3:12-CV-5141-L (2013) case be dismissed with prejudice, with all parties bearing their respective litigation costs. Farrell forced Dobbs into a traffic stop because he claimed she and her niece were littering on the highway. During the stop, Farrell believed he smelled the scent of cannabis within the car, and after questioning Dobbs, he called for backup. Helleson arrived on scene in order to execute warrantless cavity searches of both women, which included inserting her fingers inside both the anuses and vaginas of these woman; keep in mind too that Helleson used the same glove for the entirety of these searches. All of this was captured on Farrell's dashcam.

The contesting parties entered into an agreed stipulation of dismissal with prejudice because they had reached an initially undisclosed settlement. Later that day after the close of the case, Scott Palmer, the Dobbs' attorney, told a CBS affiliate in the Dallas-Fort Worth area that the settlement was in the amount of $185,000 from the Texas Department of Public Safety (DPS). I guess the lesson to be learned here then, is, don't litter while driving through Texas, because you just might get finger raped by DPS. Too bad Dobbs didn't push for a jury trial, because it would have been more satisfying for me if the jury had convicted Helleson of sexual assault and Farrell of aiding and abetting, unless that would be more appropriate for a criminal case.

Speaking of settlements, such was also the result in Eckert v. Hidalgo & Deming, No. 1:13-CV-00727 (2014) case. Eckert was forced into a traffic stop, and during the course of it, the cops lied by claiming that Eckert was hiding illicit narcotics within his anus. Eckert was subsequently arrested, and then taken to Gila Regional Medical Center, where he was forcibly anally probed repeatedly; this entailed two X-rays, three enemas, and a surgical colonoscopy. Ultimately, Eckert settled for $1,600,000 from both Hidalgo County and the City of Deming.

Interestingly enough, the settlement mentioned that Eckert must bear the cost of his own legal counsel, and is also liable for paying federal income tax. This raises a rather interesting question – are settlements, or even damages, tax exempt from federal income tax liability? If not, then that would suggest the abused citizen gets raped twice: first, by the rape itself, and secondly, by way of taxation.

Judge Edward Lodge ordered in the Miller v. City of Post Falls, No. 2:13-cv-00517-EJL (2014) case that the lawsuit be dismissed with prejudice because the parties had reached an undisclosed settlement. According to the complaint, Miller was raided in the middle of the night by the Post Falls Police Department. Office Uhrig ran up to her home, bursted through the front door, and informed Miller he was going to search her house. Despite her objection, he grabbed her arm, twisted it up behind her back, kneed her in the middle of her back, and then handcuffed her while telling her to "stop resisting." Next, Uhrig drew his gun and searched the house while repeatedly yelling, "POST FALLS POLICE DEPARTMENT!," and "GROW!," despite the hysterical shrieking of children in the home.

Requests to the officers on scene to shut the door because of the 23 degree outside weather, or to be quieter because of the sleeping infant baby, went unheeded. Miller was placed under arrest for growing cannabis, and the rest of the household were either placed into "protective custody" or were otherwise evicted from the premises. Miller was released approximately 48 hours later; 6 months later, a court hearing was set, on the grounds that she was charged with simple possession of cannabis, yet, the court ended up suppressing all evidence because the government police had made an unlawful entry.

As part of her lawsuit, Miller was ordered by the court to submit to a Defense Psychological Exam. Following the undisclosed results of that exam, the parties reach a similarly undisclosed settlement. It's awfully too bad that neither the corporate nor the alternative media were able to discover the settlement amount.

Uniquely, a jury found in the Genovese v. Town of Southampton, No. 10-CV-3470 (2014) case that malicious prosecution had occurred. Nancy Genovese was detained for over 5 hours at the side of the road because she was photographing a displayed helicopter shell at a National Guard base. Genovese's legally stored rifle was seized from her car, and she was threatened with being charged as a terrorist in order to specifically intimidate other Tea Partiers; also, defamatory statements were made about her by the government police to the mainstream press.

According to the complaint, the cops also stole $5,300 from Genovese's wallet, she was forced to disrobe in front of one of them while getting a medical examination, and they eventually put her on suicide watch, which required her to wear a suicide gown (this is essentially what mental patients in a padded room wear); despite her continued pleas for a clean gown once it had become soiled over the course of several days of being forcibly bound, these pleas went unheeded. Thankfully, the jury verdict found Deputy Robert Carlock guilty of malicious prosecution, yet, for whatever reason, they also thought that Genovese had failed to prove either battery or political oppression. The jury only awarded Genovese $1,112,000 for compensatory damages, but nothing for punitive damages against Carlock, simply because they could not reach a unanimous decision.

Judge Jeffrey White ruled in the Jewel v. NSA, No. 08-04373 (2015) case that plaintiffs had failed to establish "a sufficient factual basis…[that] they have standing to sue under the Fourth Amendment regarding the possible interception of their Internet communications." Former AT&T technician Mark Klein's testimony was useless, because he could not determine "the content, function, or purpose" of Room 641A as a black room within the SBC Communications building in San Francisco. Again, plaintiffs' case was dismissed since they were unable to challenge the constitutionality of the wiretapping because it was a dragnet, just like 8 years previously.

Tabulating these cases briefly, I think, will concisely reveal some much needed truths regarding the effectiveness of suing the government. Assuming that settlements are draws, awarded damages are wins, and dismissals with prejudice are losses, then the results of the aforementioned data set are as follows:

- ❖ ACLU: lost
- ❖ Oberwetter: lost
- ❖ Dobbs: draw
- ❖ Eckert: draw
- ❖ Miller: draw
- ❖ Genovese: won
- ❖ Jewel: lost

Out of this sample of 7 cases, in terms of percentages, this means that only 14% of these cases were clearly won, and that 42% of these cases ended equally in either a loss or a draw. Even if I inflate the success ratio by considering draws the same as wins, then still only 57% of these cases ended in some sort of monetary awards, which could be considered a viable goal for the plaintiffs if the goal was simply financial recompense, and not necessarily any serious attempt to reign in government power.

What does all of this actually mean, though? First, let's take a look at the seldom mentioned Seventh Amendment:

"In suits at common law, where the value in controversy shall exceed twenty dollars, the right of trial by jury shall be preserved, and no fact tried by a jury shall be otherwise re-examined in any Court of the United States, than according to the rules of the common law."

Obviously, it's a little hard for plaintiffs to exercise the 7th Amendment with the federal judiciary if they end up, quite literally, settling nearly all the time (pun intended), as Angel Dobbs, David Eckert, and Melissa Miller did. I fail to see how settling with the King's guards reigns in the absolute power of the State. Secondly, consider the following YouTube comments by a user, dodgeman7909, who criticized Larken Rose for being a self-defense advocate:

"Now I am a police officer but I'll be the first to tell you there are some bad cops out there but an overwhelming majority of us are good. I believe in the constitution and everybody's rights. I am against gun bans and very restricting laws. If you are too then state it and try to change it….not by saying shoot police, because that is the dumbest thing anyone could say. If you feel you are mistreated or denied your rights file a lawsuit or whatever but putting a video like this out there is ridiculous. If I had someone who tried to shoot me because they didn't believe in government or whatever it will not end well for them because my main goal everyday I go to work is to go home when I get off and I'll do anything to make that happen… And you [Larken Rose] are an extremist." [emphasis added]

If indeed this "dodgeman" is part of the gendarmerie, and a "good" one to boot, then the only remaining question would be is that, is he the exception or the rule when it comes to "good" unconstitutional policing? Notice also the quick use of the term, "extremist;" doesn't that mimic the political oppression of Nancy Genovese? Unjust profiling, much?

Let's also consider some other factors that reformists, who advocate for suing the pants off of the government, frequently ignore. Policemen and judges enjoy qualified immunity and judicial immunity, respectively. Contrasting this with the statements of "dodgeman" suggests that you must rely on the government's own rules to hold itself accountable, even if the judge ends up dismissing the case later, quite possibly with negative repercussions toward yourself if he deems the case "frivolous," or worse, declares you to be a "vexatious litigant" for even taking your case to court in the first place.

If we are to learn from the government's own example, then several more revelations present themselves for our remedial political education. Essentially, you have to wait around until the government hurts you, personally; should you receive a settlement or damages, the government will pay you using taxpayer money, or otherwise from some other source of wealth than it can easily replenish because of its taxing "authority." At most, the State is only embarrassed by the notoriety caused by a lawsuit in the corporate media, not the substance of the lawsuit itself. If what happened to a plaintiff is horrendous enough, the government will be more than happy to offer a sacrifice in order to distance its legitimacy away from your case, usually under the auspices of "this is just an isolated incident," as what happened in the Dobbs case with the firing of Helleson.

One reason to maintain as good health as possible is that once you are arrested as a political prisoner, then you are denied medical attention you ask for, and whatever medical attention they force upon you, is always used against you somehow (as in the Eckert and Genovese cases). The repeated theme in these lawsuits of narcotics prohibition, especially of cannabis (as in the Dobbs and Miller lawsuits), wouldn't be tolerated for a moment in a truly free society.

The efficacy of lawsuits is approaching that of jury nullification, quite frankly, and not just in the sense of uselessly waiting around, but also the fact that you are still reliant upon the bar attorneys to make the opportunity for these techniques to manifest themselves in the first place! There is absolutely no semblance of trying to escape from the system here, but rather, an attempt to "change the system from within" by not only embarrassing it, but also "making it pay" using other people's money, namely the taxpayers. I have not seen ONE civil case where a government cop was forced to perform restitution to his victim from his own pockets. Socializing losses, much?

Opportunity costs abound in lawsuits against the government. Civil lawsuits usually take months or even years (the Genovese case took 4 and ½ years!); imagine the emotional stress involved while the case is being adjudicated over that period of time. Should you win, consider also the opportunity costs incurred when you are doing things like reading law, talking to your lawyer, and waiting around in courtrooms. These occur even if you do "win" and receive money from the government, because that's time and effort you can't ever get back.

Worst of all, suing the government reinforces the legitimacy of the State itself. Lawsuits legitimize the coercive monopoly that is the judiciary. Reformists prefer other people to incur opportunity costs by learning all the rules of civil procedure, instead of focusing on developing free market alternatives to replace the judiciary.

To add insult to injury, nearly all the cases I've presented (except for the ACLU, Oberwetter, and Jewel cases), inherently rely on the 14th Amendment's nefarious incorporation doctrine! Every single time a reformist suggests that a Title 42 civil lawsuit should be filed against an entity from one of the several state governments, they are invoking the forceful application of the United States Constitution against the several state constitutions, by way of the 14th Amendment. Title 42 United States Code § 1983 says, in part, that:

> "Every person who, under color of any statute, ordinance, custom, or usage, of any State or Territory or the District of Columbia, subjects, or causes to be subjected, any citizen of the United States or other person within the jurisdiction thereof to the deprivation of any rights, privileges, or immunities secured by the Constitution and laws, shall be liable to the party injured in an action at law, suit in equity, or other proper proceeding for redress, except that in any action brought against a judicial officer for an act or omission taken in such officer's judicial capacity, injunctive relief shall not be granted unless a declaratory decree was violated or declaratory relief was unavailable." [emphasis added]

To be "within the jurisdiction thereof" might as well be "subject to the jurisdiction thereof," as far as I can figure it, unless there's a legalistic distinction between the word "within" and the words "subject to." You can never tell with lawyers how they are going to mangle the plain English language this week. In other words, reformists are morons who willfully neglect to read law.

The only real exception to my hypothesis that suing the government does not work is that, if what the government did to you was particularly egregious, and they impoverished you in the process, then a civil lawsuit might be your only plausible recourse towards getting your life back on track, but again, this is, at best, just a rearguard action (much like jury nullification) where the goal is to simply recoup your losses so you are not completely destitute, but it is certainly not a method you want to rely on as part of some overall strategy to secure your liberty.

Again, the best case scenario I can perceive is that the settlement or damages awarded to you make you potentially liable for paying federal income taxes, presumably because the IRS assumes the monies are the equivalent of "windfall profits," and in that sense, are much like a capital gains tax. In other words, the government still wins, thereby making "successful" grassroots lawsuits more of a Pyrrhic victory, than anything else. Sometimes when you "win," you still end up losing, simply because it's not a tactical victory, since at the end of the day, you don't come out ahead of the government in any real way, much less any sort of decisive or even strategic victories, that is, real victories.

Once you comprehend the truth that the law is a racket, then you begin to understand why really any sort of legalistic solution, unless it helps you escape or avoid the State, is truly little else other than a notorious reformist project of some kind. If the most successful result I can find from lawsuits against the government for committing explicit political oppression resulted in only compensatory damages after over 4 years in litigation, then I think any hope of "suing for freedom," much like the freedom suits of old, should be given up entirely. The fact of the matter is that America is a police state, and anybody wasting time in a government monopoly courtroom attempting to hold statists "accountable," is just as naïve or delusional as "copblockers," at this point.

If for whatever reason anyone wants to bother with suing government agents, might I suggest exploring "your" state government's laws for doing so, such as the Texas Civil Practice and Remedies Code? At least that way, you won't be invoking the 14thAmendment, and therefore it would be consistent with the legal concept of state citizenship. And for goodness' sake, fund your own legal (mis)adventures, instead of trying to socialize it onto others through activist legal defense fund scams.

When it comes to the efficacy of suing the government, I think what I have discovered here just reinforces to me that Gustave de Molinari really was correct about the privatization of security services, especially considering that these rampant abuses committed by government police would never be tolerated by the customers of privately produced security, because they would be able to boycott those corrupt producers right into bankruptcy, and rightfully so.

In summation, when a reformist is grandstanding that you aren't being patriotic enough or in accordance with libertarian principles if you fail to file a lawsuit, tell them, politely, to just bugger off. These nincompoops have failed to bear their burden of proof that lawsuits systematically work to restore or otherwise secure one's liberty. Maybe if they spent half of their advocacy time on using the economic means of making money, then perhaps they would realize that the political means of making money only leads us down to the road to perdition.

[Postscript: I'd like to thank Tennessee Rose for her invaluable assistance in getting the court documents that are now currently hosted and available for free download on Liberty Under Attack, for without her, this article would have been impossible.]

The Activist Legal Defense Fund Scam

[September 2nd, 2013]

During times of oppression, it is not at all uncommon for absolute governments to arbitrarily imprison their own people, especially those who are politically incorrect. Although such governments may not be able to openly persecute these political prisoners, they are more than happy to play the "gotcha" game by trying to arrest those individuals who violate mala prohibita (or sometimes, they'll just go ahead and frame them for it). Today, America, the purported "land of the free," enjoys the unique distinction of maintaining the largest prison population on the entire planet.

A trend I've noticed over the years is for both patriots and libertarians to elicit sympathy from their respective audiences by requesting them to support an incarcerated person whom they claim is being targeted by the government. All sorts of noise gets made (especially over digital "social" media websites like Facebook, Twitter, and YouTube), covering the details about the purported injustice being committed. At the end of the day, though, what was actually accomplished by all the yammering, ranting, and pontificating regarding the latest caged dissident?

One common aphorism promulgated by activists (who insist that others must join in their effort to provide legal defense support for a fellow jailed dissident) is by asserting that through creating "awareness" in the mainstream media about a specific prisoner, then any sort of injustice flowing from the bench would be automatically tempered by the glaring lens of the corporate media. This is fallaciously wrong on multiple counts. First, writing a letter to the editor on the prisoner's behalf is ill conceived because writing letters to the editor about any topic at all simply does not work. Second, spreading hyperlinks to articles detailing the ongoing saga to your associates and various email lists is ineffective, because how do you expect those who happen to read them to act on the information? Third, volunteering any labor, such as by writing letters to the prisoner himself, or even going so far as to attend his trial, is utterly fruitless. There is nothing you can tell the inmate that the prison guards would not also know, and unless you are testifying in court on the defendant's behalf, there is no benefit you can provide for him by simply acting as a spectator in the courtroom.

What about donating your hard-earned "Monopoly money" for the goal of helping the prisoner regain his freedom? Now we are starting to get at the heart of the matter, for "awareness" by itself does not pay the bills, as it were. Legal defense funds are all the rage in activist circles, for they seem to be a concrete way of supporting a prisoner's ability to legally defend himself in court from the government's charges. The key question that nearly all the advocates of such legal defense funds desperately attempt to avoid is, how are the funds being allocated, exactly? It is problematic regardless of whether the funds are sent to a third-party organization managing the fund, or are directly handled by the accused.

Let us first see if it is possible to determine what precisely would need to be paid out of a legal defense fund. It is not unreasonable to assume that the highest priority for any legal defense fund to pay for would be a privately hired defense attorney, who is assumed to be noticeably better at defending clients than the public defenders are (unless you believe Jim Hogshire, in which case this potential reason can be safely ruled out). Other reasons would include hiring freelance investigative reporters, or private detectives, to work undercover by trying to determine whether or not government corruption would be at play, for if it were, then the public revelation of such malfeasance would positively demonstrate that the prisoner's due process was being violated, which might be more than enough reason for all the charges against him to be dropped. **The chief goal of any legal defense fund is to hire a team of specialists who can increase the probability of either getting the defendant found innocent in court, or forcing the government's charges to be dropped completely.**

If no attorney, investigative reporter, private detective, or any other kind of legal "professional" is not having their services retained by a legal defense fund, then it does beg the question as to what those funds are being allocated towards instead. Should a defendant continue to use his court-appointed public defender, would it then be unreasonable for us to assume that any donations to such a fund are not being allocated towards any kind of legal defense (despite the fact that the prisoner in question is still asking sympathetic strangers for donations to his legal defense fund)? Is it really that strange, under these circumstances, to assume that all public requests for donations to any such "legal defense funds" are, in reality, just scams?

Luke Rudkowski, the figurehead for We Are Change, Inc., solicited for donations intended for a legal defense fund during March of 2009, on behalf of himself and two other We Are Change members, and retained all the contributions after the charges that warranted the legal defense fund were dropped. Case details provided by the New York State Unified Court System showed that Rudkowski retained the services of The Legal Aid Society (specifically the New York County Criminal Defense Office, located on 49 Thomas Street in Manhattan), whose own mission statement says that the Society is a "not-for-profit legal services organization." Rudkowski was able to raise $4,241.55 through an online ChipIn fundraiser, although none of these funds have been accounted for, as required by the We Are Change Code of Conduct; as such, there is no reason to believe that any of these funds ever made it to The Legal Aid Society (or even should have been collected in the first place).

Adam Kokesh, following the events of his arrest at Smoke Down Prohibition V on May 18th of 2013, was interviewed by We Are Change, Inc. on May 30th. He asserted that the reason the government dropped their case against him (but not against N.A. Poe for exactly the same thing, which was a felony charge for ostensibly violating Title 18, United States Code § 111) was because of his popularity on the Internet. He went on to thank George Donnelly for managing his legal defense fund, a service Kokesh described as part of his "arrest insurance" that he purchased from Donnelly (since Kokesh was a client of Shield Mutual). Kokesh also suggested that the reason N.A. Poe got railroaded by the government (and thus is still in legal limbo) was because he capitulated to "working within the system" by paying bail and so forth, thus (according to Kokesh) all of "us" need to "resist" more, which will then "force the government to back off" because the costs of enforcement would become too high for them. Worst of all, Luke Rudkowksi also recommended during this interview that in order to be "true to yourself," you must relinquish whatever privacy you have left and become a self-made public figure, lest you make yourself vulnerable to government persecution by suffering the same fate as Brandon Raub.

George Donnelly (who upon hearing that Kokesh was not going to hire a defense attorney), published an article on June 5th announcing that Shield Mutual will be offering refunds to any donators who asked for one, just as long as they do so before the two-week deadline ended on June 19th (he had raised $5,377.44 for Kokesh's legal defense fund by this point). Kokesh was subsequently arrested again, this time on June 8th at the Smoke Down Prohibition Joint Summit with President Choom in Washington DC, and then yet again on July 9th when his home was invaded at night by both Herndon and US Park Police.

Donnelly published another article on July 17th, providing screenshots of the accounting he was tasked with keeping. According this article, the amount of refunded donations, plus the payment processor's fees, came to $465.83, which left a balance of $4,911.61 in the legal defense fund, as of June 21st. This amount was sent by Donnelly to Lucas Jewell (who was Kokesh's business manager for Adam v. The Man [AVTM] at the time) in the form of a check that same day on June 21st; also, both the Bitcoin and Litecoin donations were released simultaneously as well, in the amounts of 4.5002619 BTC and 120.5 LTC (the conversions work out to approximately $450 and $284, respectively), for a current running total of

$5,646.41. Mr. Jewell contacted Donnelly on June 26th, July 2nd, and July 5th, claiming each time that the check for $4,911.61 had not been received yet. Meanwhile, presumably acting in the best interests of his client, Donnelly requested donations on July 10th for Kokesh's legal defense fund (regarding his July 9th arrest) and raised nearly $1,400 for 3 press releases, the first one of which cost him $369 out of Shield Mutual's own petty cash (the current running total, at this point, for the legal defense fund, was $6,300.58).

On July 15th, Donnelly discovered that the payment processor had stopped the payment; apparently, the United States Postal Service (USPS) claimed on July 12th that the check was "undeliverable." That same day, Donnelly issued a new check for $5,431.58 to Jeffrey Phillips (who is Kokesh's new AVTM business manager), which was $519.97 more than the previous check's amount because Donnelly wanted reimbursement for the first press release he had already issued. Also on July 15th, Donnelly gave a loan of $500 to Darrell Young (who is another AVTM staff member) for the express purpose of expediting Kokesh's bail payment; later that same day, Mr. Phillips canceled the legal defense fund (Donnelly also claimed in his July 17th articlethat $172 had been raised already, but that those donations would be refunded since Kokesh decided to use a public defender anyway).

The 5-man AVTM "business team" (composed of Darrell Young, Jeffrey Phillips, Edd Yealey, Liz Delish, and Jeremy Mazur) issued a fundraising statement on July 16th, which was read by Miss Delish:

"First of all, Adam Vs. The Man is no longer affiliated with Shield Mutual for any fundraising efforts. Please direct all of your donations to Adam Vs. The Man's page, and you can reach the 'Invest' link at http://www.adamvstheman.com/invest. At that site, you will be able to donate Bitcoin, Litecoin, and metals, as well as Federal Reserve Notes, because we wish to support alternate economies. If you have any questions whatsoever about your donation, please contact me at liz@adamvstheman.com. Tomorrow, we will be having a moneybomb fundraiser in order to muster up the funds we'll need to stabilize and keep going at full speed…[t]he donations we gather will be used for legal AND operational expenses at Adam's discretion." [emphasis added]

Ah, isn't that rather interesting? So, AVTM admits that, despite Kokesh's earlier statements on May 30th in praise of George Donnelly's management of the legal defense fund, he is still being thrown under the bus for no good reason whatsoever (as I have just outlined). AVTM then issued another press release on July 18th where this time they tried to further justify the dropping of Shield Mutual (a video version of this press release was also read by Miss Delish):

"As of July 15th, 2013, we are no longer using Shield Mutual for any of their services. The reason behind this decision is based upon funds that George Donnelly raised on May 18th, 2013. These were never released to Adam and are still missing. In light of these events, we have directed all fundraising efforts through channels that the ADAM VS THE MAN team can monitor and utilize most effectively in order to quickly and accurately enact Adam's requests from the detention center. This fundraising approach allows Adam the most control over his assets while he is unlawfully incarcerated. Adam will not be using the public defender, and therefore needs to raise at least $10,000 in order to obtain appropriate counsel." [emphasis added]

No mention was made of the hiccup with the USPS (which was not Donnelly's fault), the check Donnelly issued to Mr. Phillips for $5,431.58, or the $500 loan to Mr. Young, so the claim made by the AVTM "business team" that the funds are somehow "still missing" is brought into serious doubt. Not only that, but the AVTM "business team" now wants to handle any legal defense donations themselves, to the tune of $10,000 plus, all the while claiming that Kokesh did not want to use his public defender, which directly contradicts what Donnelly said the day before on July 17th. So, the real question here is, did Jeffrey Phillips in fact receive the check for $5,431.58 (and Darrell Young, the $500 loan; for a grand total of $5,931.58) from George Donnelly; and, did Kokesh choose to retain his public defender, or not?

Kokesh admitted in an earlier July 8th, 2013 interview on The Alex Jones Show (which was the day before his home was invaded and he was arrested yet again) that, since his open carry march into DC lacked the "critical mass" of individuals he wanted, coupled with his arrest on May 18th in Philadelphia during Smoke Down Prohibition V, it would not be wise for him to continue organizing an event that required marchers to cross a political border armed. This formed the basis for why he changed his mind from organizing a single armed march into DC on July 4th to instead propose to his audience that they should hold their own protest demonstrations at their respective state capitols. Despite this, Kokesh also said during this interview that he still wants to do the exact same march next year on Independence Day of 2014! Needless to say, that just might be impossible for him to pull off if he is convicted of the various drug and gun felony charges that is the government's justification for his July 9th arrest. Regardless of whether he is convicted, I have no doubt his AVTM "business team" will, in the meantime, rake in a handsome profit.

Unlike Adam Kokesh, N.A. Poe did provide at least a partial accounting for his legal defense fund. As you can no doubt tell from his Fundly.com page, Mr. Poe was able to raise $3,370.00 from 124 donators, whose (statistical) mode donation was $10 per donator. Unfortunately, there is absolutely no proof currently available to demonstrate what exactly Mr. Poe spent that money on; this is especially disconcerting when combined with the fact that despite my offer to him to get his story out, he has steadfastly refused to provide me with the legal documents of his case. This deeply concerns me further since he already admitted to me that the feds have attempted to turn him into an informant at least a few times now.

Charles Dyer was a former US Marine who became a vlogger and public speaker at Tea Party events. J. Croft probably describes him the best:

"Charles Dyer, otherwise known as July4Patriot [aka J4P], one of the greatest spokesmen of the real Patriot Movement, got hooked by a vindictive ex-wife, a corrupt Podunk Oklahoma town, and the FBI. It took three jury trials, but [it took] bogus child molestation charges, [as well as] his shyster court officer lawyer [who] sold him out, [that] got [him] convicted. He's serving 30 years, but [I] believe it was for his peaceable Patriot activism."

In the context of what he thinks is an example of failed legal defense support, J. Croft elaborates:

"Charles Dyer…was a Marine who spoke out during the Bush years, got in trouble for it, went to trial three times over [regarding] a bogus airsoft copy of a grenade launcher and totally made up child molestation charges, the last [of which] they won by making him flee for his life when his home and all his exculpatory evidence was burned in an act of arson-and the judge only gave him a week delay as his trial was going to start the next Monday from [when] the incident [occurred]. He fled, was sold out by his contacts, [and] was caught shirtless in Texas trying to get a drink at a restaurant. Dyer's final trial was basically one day, held mostly in the judge's chambers, and [then] he was sent to prison for 30 years. This author attempted repeatedly to rally support for Dyer, but was stymied at every turn by COINTEL operators like 'mamaliberty' and, probably worse, endemic indifference."

But is that the totality of what really happened to Charles Dyer? Was this really just a simple case of "endemic indifference," as J. Croft put it, or is there more to this story? As it turns out, there is quite a bit more than J. Croft's overly simplified, albeit well-intentioned, explanation of Dyer's legal saga.

Debra Swan established the Dollars4Dyer legal defense fund in September of 2011. After Miss Swan had collected only $50 in donations, Rick Light committed libel when he asserted that she stole $10,000 from the fund, as well as claiming that Jan Dyer (Charles' mother) never had access to the funds raised, or was even aware of it (this is also the very same Rick Light who has been consorting with employees or agents of the government, especially the FBI with regard to the Charles Dyer affair). Concurrently, a totally separate legal defense fund was established on ChipIn by Patriot Unity Coalition member organization Patriot Legal Defense (that has since become defunct), which was run by Nancy Genovese (aka, Mystcstar), who was the very same individual who single-handedly bankrolled New Colony Media during my short-lived stint with them. No accounting of any donated funds was ever made publicly available by Genovese's Patriot Legal Defense organization.

Similar to Rick Light's libel against Miss Swan, Randy Mack was slandered by Jim Stach, who asserted that not only had Randy tried "to destroy J4P's donations," but also that Randy had accused Jim himself of having the means to access the PayPal account, through which Jim supposedly stole an undefined amount of donations (of course, since it has already been established that there were at least two completely separate legal defense funds for Charles Dyer, it is still unclear which fund Jim was referring to in his slander against Randy).

When Chris Mortenson, a former US Marine, hired the US Observer to perform some investigative reporting about Charles Dyer's legal troubles, Ed Snook breached his contract by simultaneously contracting with Jan Dyer and Amy Dark (Charles' sister) for the exact same work (to the tune of $6,500 and $3,000; respectively), as well as committing libel and slander against not only Mr. Mortenson but also Miss Swan, the latter of whom actually signed the contract on Mortenson's behalf, since he was simply bankrolling Snook's assignment to the tune of a $10,000 retainer, for a grand total of $19,500.00 that the US Observer was paid. Granted, while there was no formal legal defense fund involved here, one of the key purposes (as I stated earlier) for why you have such a fund in the first place is to hire legal "professionals" (like Mr. Snook) to get the defendant off the hook. I don't think it is too much of a stretch to assume that all the money paid out by Mr. Mortenson, Mrs. Dyer, and Mrs. Dark, for the express purpose of vindicating Charles Dyer, would be, in reality, fundamentally different from what any legal defense fund is supposed to accomplish (and at the very least, it still qualifies as legal defense support). Any investigative expose about Charles Dyer's legal troubles shouldn't have to cost almost $20,000 to write up.

Examining the legal defense funds and "support work" involving Luke Rudkowski, Adam Kokesh, and Charles Dyer reveals some pretty ugly facts. First, there is no way of measuring how effective "spreading awareness" about some random dissident's legal troubles actually is. Second, non-monetary legal defense support (such as writing letters to the editor, or attending court hearings) are worse than useless, because they are counter-productive methods that necessarily increase opportunity costs. Third, private defense attorneys are almost never actually hired, even though this is the primary reason for a legal defense fund in the first place. Fourth, any accounting of the donations is rarely ever provided, either privately to each of the donators, or publicly; if anyone should demand financial transparency (as was the case with some of the We Are Change members, like Louie Bee), or themselves release the transaction records (as was the case with George Donnelly), they are harshly demonized by those individuals and "circled wagon crews" who seek to benefit from the naïveté of well-meaning donators (or alternatively, the "circled wagon crews" will attempt to deflect attention from themselves by falsely accusing other individuals of stealing from the legal defense funds, as what happened to Debra Swan and Randy Mack). This naïveté does not come cheap, as it has cost donators (cumulatively from the three case studies already covered) to the tune of at least $29,673.13 (granted, this pales in comparison to Ron Paul's phony 2012 presidential electoral bid, which is estimated to be a whopping $40 million, but I digress).

What can be done about this, if anything? Let us consult J. Croft again:

> "Common gangbangers can count on support for their trial and [while] in prison. When they get out [of prison], they are not [out] on their ass. That the Patriot Movement could learn from street thugs is by itself testament enough to how ineffective the 'movement' has been led to be. It's a testament to how the 'movement' has been left in the hands of celebrity gatekeepers who effectively neutralize it for the enemy."

In other words, political dissidents suffer from less camaraderie than even street gangs do. As such, when your time comes, you will experience it totally and completely alone, whether it be a brief roadside detention, a longer-term incarceration, or even the morgue (at least, absent a security team, anyway). Should you and I take the no-so-subtle hint that the "teasing the bear" variety of civil disobedience does not work either?

Might it be preferable to instead practice discrete civil disobedience, like SEK3 advocated?

But what if you feel that you must donate? In that case, I would most strongly suggest that you perform your own due diligence and ask the legal defense fund manager(s) whether they have retained the services of an attorney, or not. If they haven't found one yet because they're "still considering" whom they'd like to represent the defendant, than that should be an automatic red flag for you; in that case, I think you should react by delaying on donating anything until such time an attorney is retained (if it happens at all). If you have learned instead that the defendant has decided to use his public defender (or chosen to represent himself), then the need to donate to a legal defense fund is rendered moot. If a lawyer has been retained, but you are uncomfortable with donating money to the legal defense fund (because of the fund's manager, for instance), then I would advise you to pay the lawyer directly, if at all possible.

Holding a moneybomb fundraiser vis-à-vis a crowdfunding website on behalf of the accused does not solve the abovementioned problems with the systematic lack of transparency, either. Whether it be sites like Kickstarter, IndieGoGo, or Patreon, the trend appears to be, generally speaking, against showing what those donations were spent on (as was the case with N.A. Poe mentioned earlier). Until such time those expenses are shared publicly (in emulation of George Donnelly), or at least made available to the donators themselves, I wouldn't put much faith in the reliability of any of these so-called "legal defense fund managers" to be responsible with the collected monies.

Regardless of which option you take, do it for the right reasons; don't do it because you've been guilt tripped by the empty rhetoric emanating from the mouth of some manipulative talking head. You are not a bad person and your ideals are not rendered somehow insincere because you didn't bend over and immediately donate money to a random legal defense fund for someone you either don't know, or have reservations about. On the other hand, if you avoid performing your own due diligence and just flippantly donate to a legal defense fund because some self-important Internet political pundit with delusions of grandeur demanded you to do so, then you have nobody to blame but yourself. In that case, you chose to assume full and total responsibility for your actions by being willing to literally gamble your money on whether the legal defense fund managers have the integrity to allocate the funds for what they advertised they'd be used for, instead of being diverted under false pretenses to someone's personal kiddie fund.

There is, of course, a much simpler, yet absolutist, route you could take. Just simply ignore any and all public requests for donations to legal defense funds carte blanche. Save your money and use it for whatever you would've otherwise have donated towards something that can actually help you secure your Liberty (like buying a carton of bullets, for instance). Don't just stop there, though; I further recommend you don't waste your time and effort rampantly consuming all the nitty gritty details about some random "liberty activist" who got arrested by the government during this week's news cycle, like I have in the past (as demonstrated by the three copiously detailed aforementioned case studies about Rudkowski, Kokesh, and Dyer). There is virtually nothing to be learned from their escapades, other than what not to do. If you sincerely want to learn about what you should do, I recommend you do yourself a favor (and lower your opportunity costs) by reading You Are Going to Prison, and applying Jim Hogshire's advice as you need it. The old adage, "An ounce of prevention is worth a pound of cure," is never more true than when you are evading and/or attempting to survive the beast that is the American criminal (in)justice system.

Just as survivalists have bug out plans, I believe it is imperative for all American political dissidents from across the entire ideological spectrum to devise what the copblockers have described as an "arrest plan." Namely, it would be prudent to make arrangements before you experience a police interrogation to have any dependents of yours squirreled away with someone trustworthy, to inform a single point of contact that you are being held by government police, and to shower and shave for your mug shot (if at all possible), regardless of whether the scenario is a roadside traffic stop, or a midnight home raid. Of course, you could negate any purported need for legal defense funds if you approach your legal troubles from the perspective of a state citizen (such as by acting as a pro se litigant, having someone you trust act as "next friend," or filing a habeas corpus ad subjiciendum to challenge the legality of your incarceration), then legal defense funds become moot, unless you seriously want to beg perfect strangers to foot the bill for your own court costs. Similarly, if you've allocated some of your savings ahead of time towards future commissary purchases, then any excuses to jimmy up requests for donations gets reduced down to zero.

I guess the biggest problem I have with the whole notion of volunteering my personal time to provide legal defense "support," or worse, donating my hard-earned Monopoly money to a shady legal defense fund, is that the entire concept is predicated on the assumption that if the "we" support the prisoner's attempt to legally "work within the system," then that is the only realistic chance he has for regaining his freedom. The unsaid justification behind legal support work (with or without a concomitant defense fund) is inherently reformist; it relies on the beast's own rules to escape the clutches of the beast itself (such "rules" intrinsically violate any notion of due process, procedural or substantive). Besides, do you want to be responsible for justifying the existence and actions of the American Bar Association through your funding of its attorneys?

In summation, giving free legal defense support, or donating to a legal defense fund, is a recipe for failure. Consider also that the oh-so-valuable bar attorney is bound by the rules of the court which unfairly favors the Administrative Agencies, anyway (if you don't believe me, then read Justice Brandeis' concurring opinion in Ashwander v. TVA). Generally speaking, it costs a minimum of $20,000 to legally contest criminal charges successfully, and the ones who stand to gain the most from it (aside from the scumbag bar attorneys) are the notorious patriots-for-profit. They nickel and dime their audiences for such lesser stuff, and thus bleed them dry slowly over time. All they want are Federal Reserve Notes; have you noticed that they never seem to accomplish anything substantive (much how like the American Cancer Society claims to want to cure cancer)? The whole idea of legal defense support is literally stupid, both deontologically as well as in a utilitarian sense; the presumption it has of "leave no one behind" is bullshit, plain and simple. An individual soldier is expendable, since it would be a waste of effort to try and rescue him (either through proving his innocence in court, or by way of a operationally planned and executed prison-break). Sadly, the truth of the matter is that nobody is coming to save you from the gulag when your time comes, so act accordingly.

Jury Nullification Does Not Work

September 12th, 2014

Since time immemorial, juries have been what some have referred to as the "palladium of liberty" against tyrannical government. Long before the ratification of the United States Constitution in the late 1780s, jurors had the ability to not only be finders of fact, but also as judges of the law itself, especially as applied to a particular defendant on trial; it was the intention of the Founders that such jury nullification would act as a legal method with which to bloodlessly resist tyrants. Unfortunately, this peculiarly unique veto suffers not only from the government's secrecy about its very existence as a recognized legal doctrine, but also from the human frailty in the willingness to exercise it, both of which deeply challenge its modern efficacy in short-circuiting the cyclical theory of history.

When learning about the historicity of jury nullification, you must consider not only the verification of its deontological virtues, but also the debunking of its utilitarian value as a check and balance against the enforcement of bad government laws. Lysander Spooner wrote at length, in 1852, about how it was the right, and more importantly, the duty of jurors to judge the justice of the law; that is, it was the prerogative of the jury to judge the law itself by voting their conscience. Yet, Spooner also mentioned that the United States Congress had abrogated the responsibility of preserving jury trials over to the several state governments, thus arguing that had the federal courts preserved jury trials, as well as the citizenry remaining knowledgeable about their juror veto, then the Congress would not have been so prolific in their rampant passage of legislation, or at the very least, that such enforcement would have been greatly hampered. Although I doubt that had federal judges informed juries in their instructions to them about their power to nullify that would have somehow hindered the passage of congressional legislation, I do think that Spooner was correct about the ignorance of Americans on their ability to nullify unjust government edicts.

Constitutionally speaking, jury nullification is implied by the right of trial by jury itself. Article III § 2 clause 3, the Fifth Amendment, the Sixth Amendment, the Seventh Amendment, and even the Ninth Amendment of the United States Constitution all say in turn, respectively, that:

"The Trial of all Crimes, except in Cases of Impeachment, shall be by Jury; and such Trial shall be held in the State where the said Crime shall have been committed..."

"No person shall be held to answer for a capital, or otherwise infamous crime, unless on a presentment or indictment of a Grand Jury..."

"In all criminal prosecutions, the accused shall enjoy the right to a speedy and public trial, by an impartial jury of the State and district wherein the crime shall have been committed..."

"In suits at common law, where the value in controversy shall exceed twenty dollars, the right of trial by jury shall be preserved, and no fact tried by a jury shall be otherwise re-examined in any Court of the United States, then according to the rules of the common law."

"The enumeration in the Constitution, of certain rights, shall not be construed to deny or disparage others retained by the people."

Explicitly mentioned no less than five times, considering also the scope of the unenumerated rights, really demonstrates the point of commonality between the Federalists and Anti-Federalists during the ratification period. According to the current Texas Constitution of 1876, Article I §§ 10, 8, and 2 say, respectively, that:

"In all criminal prosecutions the accused shall have a speedy public trial by an impartial jury."

"And in all indictments for libels, the jury shall have the right to determine the law and the facts, under the direction of the court, as in other cases."

"The faith of the people of Texas stands pledged to the preservation of a republican form of government, and, subject to this limitation only, they have at all times the inalienable right to alter, reform, or abolish their government in such manner as they may think expedient."

Obviously, a government that recognizes the right of revolution should also recognize, to paraphrase Tom Stahl, jury nullification as an expression of such alteration and reformation of the government.

Statutorily, however, the federal government mandates jury duty from the American citizenry in Title 28, United States Code §§ 1861 – 1869;

the Texan government similarly requires jury duty from its citizens pursuant to Chapter 62 of the Texas Government Code, as well as from Article 19 within the Texas Code of Criminal Procedure. Qualified jurors are defined by the federal government in 28 USC § 1865, and by the Texan government in Article 19.08; in brief, both governments define law-abiding adult citizens of sound mind who comprehend English to be, more or less, potential jurors. Failure to respond to a jury summons, however, is punishable by 28 USC § 1866(g) and §§ 62.0141 & 62.111 of the Texas Government Code, respectively, as:

"Any person summoned for jury service who fails to appear as directed may be ordered by the district court to appear forthwith and show cause for failure to comply with the summons. Any person who fails to show good cause for noncompliance with a summons may be fined not more than $1,000, imprisoned not more than three days, ordered to perform community service, or any combination thereof."

"In addition to any criminal penalty prescribed by law, a person summoned for jury service who does not comply with the summons as required by law or who knowingly provides false information in a request for an exemption or to be excused from jury service is subject to a contempt action punishable by a fine of not less than $100 nor more than $1,000."

"A juror lawfully notified shall be fined not less than $100 nor more than $500 if the juror: (1) fails to attend court in obedience to the notice without reasonable excuse; or (2) files a false claim of exemption from jury service."

Although the right of trial by jury, and jury nullification by implication, are constitutionally guaranteed by both governments, the cost of that enjoyment is the statutory threat of punishment against brazenly disobedient citizens ranging anywhere from a minimum $100 fine to a maximum penalty of three days incarceration, a $1,000 fine, and a unknown number of hours of unpaid labor, depending on which government you're dealing with; needless to say, civilly disobeying a jury summons is not without the risk of potential jail time.

Does a citizens' grand jury enjoy any nullification abilities? Perhaps, but if any citizens' grand jury were to be convened, I doubt it would be respected or even tolerated by the government. Consider the ramifications of the 1996 Tampa Common Law Court Trial had on the lives of Philip Marsh, Emilio Ippolito, and especially, Larry Myers. Although the Under One Banner petition I signed last year does demand that the United States

Congress pass legislation to empanel a federal Citizens' Grand Jury with the explicit purpose of hearing charges on violations of the United States Constitution (pursuant to Art. III §§ 1 & 8, as an "inferior court"), this was intended more as an olive branch to demonstrate that the federal government cares absolutely nothing for you, as further evidenced by the standard form letter I received from U.S. Senator John Cornyn.

In light of the two classes of American citizenship, what would constitute a jury of your peers? If the jury pool is nearly composed entirely of 14th Amendment citizens, by what right does a United States citizen have to sit in judgement of a Citizen of a State? The Handbook for Federal Grand Jurors neglects to address this pivotal question, and neither does the Handbook for Trial Jurors Serving in the United States District Courts; as can be expected, the Texas Uniform Jury Handbook says nothing about this either.

What the governments' jury handbooks do say is more blandly procedural than anything else. Namely, that there are citizens who are eligible for jury duty, and that these qualified potential jurors are placed in the jury wheel, which randomly selects whom may be summoned. Those citizens who receive a jury summons must appear at the specified courthouse for voir dire (that is, jury selection), and that those citizens who pass muster through voir dire are sworn in as jurors. During their time as a juror, the judge will give jury instructions as to how the jurors are supposed to judge the merits of the prosecution's case against the defendant. Towards the latter end of their service, the jurors retire for jury deliberation, where they privately discuss behind closed doors what happened in the courtroom, and ultimately decide the defendant's fate. When the jury has finished deliberating by voting, they reappear in the courtroom to deliver their verdict, assuming, of course, that they avoid becoming a hung jury.

Jury nullification happens when the jurors are deliberating. By either causing a hung jury or an outright acquittal, even a single juror who votes his conscience can set the accused free, or at least cause the prosecutor some grief by the judge declaring a mistrial. This is all assuming, of course, that a fully informed juror has survived the aforementioned stages in the jury process without incident, with the hardest one being voir dire, which has been used by the government to intentionally weed out anyone who is even aware of the jury's historic power to nullify unjust government laws.

World-renowned for being the most recognizable advocates of jury nullification, libertarians have garnered a reputation that has become nearly synonymous to them just as much as they are popularly recognized for being the most vocal opponents to the entire concept of the government's so-called "victimless crimes." Unfortunately, to paraphrase St. Bernard of Clairvaux, the path to hell is paved with good intentions, and the typical libertarian intention to educate potential jurors about their historic veto power, more often than not, increases their opportunity costs. Despite adhering to the same political philosophy myself, I most vehemently disagree with the faith most libertarians place in the educational outreach of jury rights.

Case in point, the mission of the Fully Informed Jury Association (FIJA) is to teach jurors about their historic, and current, legal ability to nullify tyrannical laws. Granted, they have a terrific selection of free downloadable leaflets and other educational material with which to spread the good message of jury nullification, yet I was dismayed at the email I received back from Kirsten Tynan as to the effectiveness of jury nullification in rolling back the power of government. She stuck with the two frequently cited examples of the 1850 Fugitive Slave Act and the 18th Amendment's prohibition of alcohol as unjust laws that jury nullification was effective in overturning; these examples, as well as the Whiskey rebels of 1794 and the Vietnam era draft dodgers, are the typical ones used by FIJA (as well as by most libertarians) to demonstrate the alleged effectiveness of jury nullification. Seldom has any FIJA or libertarian source used cannabis as a modern example; even then, there are rarely any specific cases that are cited where any bad law was successfully nullified by the jury since Ronald Reagan's presidency.

Oddly enough, some of the most vocal advocates of jury nullification are anarchists. Larken Rose and Josie Wales are but just two of the numerous contemporary voluntaryists who wholeheartedly endorse jury nullification. Initially, this may seem strange given that jury nullification is simply little more than a negation of government law, but then again, so is anarchism, which is simply little more than a negation of the State; in that regard, the appeal of jury nullification to anarchists makes a strange sort of sense. Unless, of course, you take Murray Rothbard's position on jury duty:

"Finally, there is another cornerstone of the judicial system which has unaccountably gone unchallenged, even by libertarians, for far too long. This is compulsory jury service. There is little difference in kind, though obviously a great difference in degree, between compulsory jury duty and conscription; both are enslavement, both compel the individual to perform tasks on the State's behalf and at the State's bidding. And both are a function of pay at slave wages. Just as the shortage of voluntary enlistees in the army is a function of a pay scale far below the market wage, so the abysmally low pay for jury service insures that, even if jury 'enlistments' were possible, not many would be forthcoming. Furthermore, not only are jurors coerced into attending and serving on juries, but sometimes they are locked behind closed doors for many weeks, and prohibited from reading newspapers. What is this but prison and involuntary servitude for noncriminals?"

Although I have pointed out before that Mr. Libertarian might as well be thought of as Mr. Voting, I believe Rothbard has hit the nail squarely on the head here. He goes on to say that:

"It will be objected that jury service is a highly important civic function, and insures a fair trial which a defendant may not obtain from the judge, especially since the judge is part of the State system and therefore liable to be partial to the prosecutor's case. Very true, but precisely because the service is vital, it is particularly important that it be performed by people who do it gladly, and voluntarily. Have we forgotten that free labor is happier and more efficient than slave labor? The abolition of jury-slavery should be a vital plank in any libertarian platform. The judges are not conscripted; neither are the opposing lawyers; and neither should the jurors."

Keeping in mind Gustave de Molinari's thesis that the free market produces better quality security services than the government, is it really that farfetched to contemplate the idea that perhaps the private production of arbitration and/or adjudication services would be preferable to what the judiciary's government-enforced monopoly on the law can provide? If so, then advocating for the use of jury nullification would be, at best, a rearguard action, at least until such time that the agorists can reliably sell private dispute resolution services to their clientele.

Why isn't jury nullification explained in school, or more often in the corporate media? As Erick Haynie remarked back in 1997:

"The great distinction in American jury nullification doctrine, however, is that while juries enjoy an unrestrained power to nullify the law, courts almost universally forbid this power to be explained to juries. The prevailing view among jurisdictions is that affirmative instruction on the ability to nullify would lead to lawlessness in the jury decision-making process...[t]hus, whatever may have been the practice of common law England or the courts of the early American Republic, modern American juries are not instructed to determine or weigh the utility or validity of the law. Although the great majority of American courts recognize the power of the jury to nullify, neither the defendant's attorney, nor the court, is typically allowed to inform the jury of that power. Judges are to instruct juries on the applicable law; juries are to apply that law to the facts of the case."

In other words, jury nullification is treated essentially as an "open secret" by the bar attorneys, much like how these lawyers have been creating their unconstitutional bureaucratic Administrative Agencies since 1946, or have conveniently ignored the existence of the Titles of Nobility Amendment. Put another way, those silly American people cannot be trusted with the awesome power of jury nullification, yet these gracious bar attorneys are oh-so-responsible in their systematic violations of the U.S. Constitution. So, unless a juror is somehow told about their (mostly) unenumerated right to judge the law as well as the facts of a case by voting their conscience before they are summoned for jury duty, jury nullification will never happen.

Unlike their failure to officially recognize the Titles of Nobility Amendment last year, the New Hampshire legislature did successfully pass a bill in June of 2012 that adds a sentence to their Revised Statutes Annotated, which is cited at RSA 519:23-a, as saying that:

> "In all criminal proceedings the court shall permit the defense to inform the jury of its right to judge the facts and the application of the law in relation to the facts in controversy."

Thankfully, the New Hampshire legislature decided to rebuke the institutional secrecy about jury nullification, at least to the degree that the defense is allowed to inform the jury of their unique veto without risking a contempt of court charge. I must ask though, does a statute like RSA 519:23-a actually make any significant difference in increasing the probability that a juror will nullify a bad law? Answering that question necessarily requires pointing out the fact that 97% of federal cases, and 94% of state cases, never arrive at trial, mainly because the defendants plea bargain out in exchange for a perceived lesser sentence.

How has FIJA's track record been over the past 20 – 30 years in educating citizens who may soon find themselves in a position to use jury nullification? Other than Julian Heicklen getting arrested by the Standing Army numerous times for simply handing out FIJA leaflets, not too much; in fact, one could argue, quite easily, that juries are all too quick to convict defendants. Consider Rich Paul, Larken Rose, or many of the defendants Harvey Silverglate wrote about; regarding Kate Ager's conviction, none other than Ian Bernard remarked:

> "So, the cops were just being ludicrous, but [the] fact is, people trust the cops, and this jury came back after 45 minutes of deliberations with a guilty verdict. They had called, I guess, to ask for the videos, so they could watch them.... as usual, whomever the holdouts were

decided to flip over to 'guilty'…. they already had lunch, but they wanted to get out, and didn't want to come back the next day, but it's just so disappointing. People are so likely to go along with the group. You could still say 'not guilty'…if you find yourself on a jury, and you find yourself in the position where you could nullify a bad law, because there's plenty of juries being selected across the country for people who have never harmed another person… then go ahead and hold out. If you know the law is bad, vote 'not guilty.' You, your one vote, could cause that mistrial, and make the state have to go through the process all over again…now, I have a friend in Florida who told me he got on a jury once recently, and he found himself in a position where he was pressured, where he broke…it's groupthink, it's peer pressure, and somebody who knew better, broke."

Even when Bernard tried on two different occasions to get a 5 minute interview with jurors by paying them $20 each, only one former juror, from what became known as the "Trespassive Three" trial, took him up on his offer. Not for attribution, she said regarding being told about jury nullification in the courtroom that:

"I do believe they [the defendants] have the right to be there [in a public park past 11 pm], but I also believe that we need to have rules in our society, and if we don't follow those rules – I was telling the people there in the jury with me, I come from a country where there are not a lot of rules, and my country is not doing very well, so I choose to follow those rules so I can leave a better country."

In terms of whether she thought constitutions can be superseded by municipal ordinances, she said it's hard to answer because (allegedly) constitutions "give us" rights, yet, those freedoms have to applied in the "right way." So, whether informed by FIJA, or the government itself, what can be extrapolated from her responses (as well as from the minimal responses from Rich Paul's jury) is that ultimately the reason why jurors do not nullify is either because they believe that, despite constitutional law, the lawyers should make the "rules" we all must obey, or, because they are incentivized to convict.

Remember what Rothbard said earlier in this article about jury duty being a form of indentured servitude? I revisit that here in order to provide a likely explanation for why jurors appear all too quick to convict defendants. The jury is just as captive as the defendant is, because both are being threatened by the government, albeit in different ways; the former via criminal charges hanging over his head, and the latter via 28 USC § 1866(g) or §§ 62.0141 & 62.111 of the Texas Government Code, as applicable. Ergo, you literally have this version on a theme of the prisoner's dilemma game, with the noticeable difference that the jury has much more power than the defendant does in determining how quickly they can escape. Should it be a surprise to anyone that the jury would choose to save themselves rather than spend one more minute than they think they have to in acquitting a defendant who may have harmed no one?

Jury nullification, if anything were to be objectively said about it, works just as well as state nullification, which is to say, not at all. The numerous barriers to entry the American governments throw up to obstruct fully informed jurors from judging the law itself by voting their conscience makes it nearly impossible for such jurors to nullify unjust government edicts. As if that wasn't bad enough, most defendants muck up their own case by plea bargaining out; and even when they don't, jurors are more likely than not to just rubber-stamp whomever the lawyers wanted railroaded straight into prison. Even if a juror successfully managed to nullify a bad law, despite everything I've just mentioned, he is still liable to be punished by the judge, as Laura Kriho was back in 1996. This inherently reformist method of telling the government where to step off, when examined in the light of hard experience, portrays a very different face of unnecessarily increased opportunity costs.

Given the aforementioned details, what should your attitude and actions be towards jury duty? Your options, as I see it, are a sliding scale in shades of grey. One option would be to follow FIJA's advice by becoming what some have called a "stealth juror" by answering the lawyers' questions during voir dire as honestly, yet vaguely, as you can. Another option would be to go ahead and obey their law by appearing in court, but then deliberately sabotaging it by saying during voir dire that you are knowledgeable about jury nullification; this would be done in order to increase the probability that you'll be dismissed from jury duty (and thus, getting back to your own life as soon as possible). As an unknown libertarian has advised:

> "If you are called to serve as a juror, stating that you are a libertarian or are familiar with the Fully Informed Juror movement will likely get you dismissed, because government wants convictions regardless of bad law or the applicability of good law. Convictions make it appear as if they are justifying their cost. Convictions are a warning to anyone who would oppose the government or its agents."

I guess that is as good advice as any when it comes to handling jury duty. Yet another route would be to unregister from the voter rolls (as I did last year) and allow your driver's license to lapse in order to avoid being put on the jury wheel. The reason you would have to do both is because the several state governments, including Texas, more often than not draw the jury pool from both the voter registration and driver's license databases; by contrast, the federal government only considers the voter registration databases maintained by the state governments for their jury wheels. Of course, there is always the civil disobedience approach whereby you would remain a registered voter and/or licensed driver, yet when summoned for jury duty, you choose to just not show up for court. Naturally, since such an act would be a brazen act of civil disobedience since you'd already be identified by law enforcement, it would only make sense to prepare yourself to suffer the punishment when the gendarmerie are sent after you.

Attempting to reclaim the jury box is long past. Sure, one could point to the successes of Pastor Stephen Anderson or Vernice Kuglin, but seriously, aren't disobeying a police officer and tax evasion still illegal? If so, then how effective were those jury acquittals in "nullifying" unjust laws, anyway? Regardless, what about Donald Scott, Michael Hill, Vicki Weaver, David Koresh, Jose Guerena, or Oscar Grant? Oh, wait, that's right...none of them ever got a chance to "have their day in court," did they? Maybe, just maybe, shouldn't Americans rely less on the State and more on their own native intuition for creatively securing their liberties, without the government's permission?

Reformism Does Not Work: A Critique of Political Activism

[July 16th, 2015]

"They tell us, sir, that we are weak – unable to cope with so formidable an adversary. But when shall we be stronger? Will it be the next week, or the next year? Will it be when we are totally disarmed, and when a British guard shall be stationed in every house? Shall we gather strength by irresolution and inaction? Shall we acquire the means of effectual resistance by lying supinely on our backs, and hugging the illusive phantom of hope, until our enemies shall have bound us hand and foot?"

– Patrick Henry

As I've written before, sound strategy rests of the rational synergy between ends and means. Diminishing the possibility of resistance by way of movement and surprise is fundamentally good strategy. Perfect strategy would produce a victory that would be virtually bloodless. Conversely, bad strategy would entail using the direct approach.

Grand strategy, therefore, necessarily requires ends-means consistency in order to have a any probability of success, in accordance with just war theory, particularly jus ad bellum. If there are no strategic goals, then what milestones could possibly ever be used to measure incrementally progressive successes? The fact of the matter is that reformism has utterly failed to satisfy its burden of proof for demonstrating its very integrity, simply because it is strategically unsound for the cause of human liberty.

Reformism, simply defined, is any attempt at working inside of the system in order to change it from within; in brief, reformism is applied collectivism. It operates on the presumption that individuals do not matter, and therefore only what the collective wants is what matters, in the final equation. Ideologues believe in the sanctity of the centrally planned tragedy of the commons, and they falsely justify the precautionary principle to shun market options as any sort of viable response to tyranny, preferring instead the empty moral platitudes of democracy.

What this means, of course, is that reformists are not only anti-philosophic, but also anti-empirical. They ridicule the twin libertarian maxims of the non-aggression principle and the self-ownership axiom, while also willfully ignoring the regulatory capture inherent to central planning, or the tragedy of the commons as a negative externality itself. Reformists, truth be told, worship their superhuman deity called "government," whenever they insist Americans are just one more law away from utopia. Worst of all, reformists have the unbelievable gall to insinuate that their critics should be dismissed out of hand because they are allegedly free riders.

For three years, I have periodically addressed some technique of reformism that promised the moon to desperate men and women seeking any remedy that might alleviate their grievances. Each and every single time, without fail, my examinations into these methods revealed the grotesque face of modern American democracy. A listed bibliography of the entire series is as follows:

- ❖ Should You Avoid the News?
- ❖ Debating Does Not Work
- ❖ Should You Write a Letter to the Editor?
- ❖ Writing Your Congressman Does Not Work
- ❖ Petitioning Does Not Work
- ❖ Voting Does Not Work
- ❖ Protesting Does Not Work
- ❖ Grassroots Lobbying Does Not Work: A Review of Chris Cantwell's "Anarcho-Lobbyist" Series (Season One)
- ❖ Running for Public Office Does Not Work: Why "Infiltrating the State" is Foolish
- ❖ Filming Government Agents Does Not Work
- ❖ Suing the Government Does Not Work: Lawsuits Are Not Useful for Securing Your Liberty
- ❖ The Activist Legal Defense Fund Scam
- ❖ Jury Nullification Does Not Work

Whether it be elections, juries, or the news cycle, I think it is more than fair to say that the efficacy of the ballot box and the jury box can be safely judged to be insufficient for restoring liberty. Although I still have some faith in the soap box as a vehicle primarily for education, I am not naïve enough to believe that the soap box alone will prevent democide, which, as the evitable end of statism, will force you, sooner or later, to choose between the immediate fate of the pine box or a chance at liberation through the ammo box.

For instance, the proliferation of alternative media websites has inadvertently promulgated a culture of gossiping and rumor-mongering. Counter-productive debates between libertarians and statists are hosted by outfits that should know better than to place these very different folks in the same room. Writing letters to congresscritters and editors of corporate newspapers not only disrespects individual privacy, but prolifically wastes the human labor invested in persuading those whom will never read such letters. Petitions for redressing grievances are systematically ignored, and no voter can rationally evaluate which candidate would become the best elected ruler.

Begging for the rulers to solve your problems while yelling like a hooligan on the streets just demonstrates (pun intended) that you don't deserve to be free, and neither does begging the rulers more politely at their own headquarters. Much like the corporate newspaper editors, politicians establish barriers to entry so as to further entrench their thrones from being challenged by hapless Americans. Government agents cannot be held accountable at all, and no amount of filming or suing them is going to change that fact. Finally, should you find yourself in legal hot water, socializing your court costs onto strangers by begging or guilt-tripping them into doing so is utterly repugnant, especially if the money is ultimately funneled towards something else entirely.

An explication about jury nullification is warranted here. Out of all the reformist techniques, jury nullification is, by far, my favorite of the bunch; yet, unlike Larken Rose, I am not at all convinced of its efficacy in securing liberty, as well as the fact that unlike every other single method I've written about, it's the only one that's coercive, mainly because of what statists call "jury duty," which uses initiatory force in fabricating a sense of legitimacy towards either condemning humans who have harmed no one, or in excessively punishing those who have committed an injury to another.

If Shane Radliff's experience in being coerced by the Illinoisan McLean County government into serving as a juror, just so he could be forced to convict a woman of "felony scratching," for which she is currently rotting away in a government dungeon for the next 4 years, tells us anything about the power of jury nullification, it would be that nullification was immaterial to her case, yet, it made Shane complicit in giving a sense of legitimacy to the State, above and beyond his objections to the whole freakshow. In light of this, what value does jury nullification have to offer us in terms of shrinking the power of the State? I'd say about as much as a habeas corpus ad subjiciendum, at this point.

Pragmatism is often touted by reformists as the sole justification for their failed methodology. Larken Rose already debunked this nearly two years ago:

"Most 'activism' is completely worthless; in fact, it's worst than completely worthless [because] it accomplishes more harm than good...I speak from experience. Many, many years ago, when I still believed in statism, I was politically active, and I campaigned, and I played those games, and I wrote my congressman, and did all that stuff (I'm kinda embarrassed to admit it now), but, yeah, I did that too. At the time, I really and truly believed that I was 'fighting the right fight,' [that] I was fighting against the beast. It only occurred to me many years later that I was actually feeding the beast lots and lots of fuel."

He's absolutely correct, particularly when you consider that reformists never measure the efficacy of their own "solutions." For all of their talk about the virtues of "playing the game," consider then how many elections have been won, how many unjust laws have been repealed, and how many cops and bureaucrats have been personally impoverished (or even fired) for their abusive corruption? I believe the right adage here would be, the silence is deafening.

The vainglory permeating reformist sophistry grows the misconceptions they perpetuate. Legal remedies such as reclaiming unclaimed property, or expatriation, are not reformist, simply because their goal is to assist dissidents in avoiding or escaping the State, as opposed to "infiltrating" it in order to remake it in their own image. Special interests (like secret societies, various flavors on the demographic kaleidoscope, "the corporations," etc.) are the convenient bogeymen touted by reformists to be the problem, instead of understanding that the real problem standing against human freedom is the idea of "authority" itself; perhaps this will make sense to you once you comprehend the fact that most conspiracists are reformists.

Contrarily, not all minarchists are reformists, yet, too many of the anarchic philosophical schools tolerate reformism. Direct action, that is, the economic means of making money, is lambasted by reformists as either impractical or dangerous. If anybody is to be accused of being limited hangouts, it would be the reformists themselves, as evidenced by Naomi Wolf's proclamation to the Free Staters during the 2014 New Hampshire Liberty Forum that, "We need the State…we need to become the State."

Everything I've done to free myself has either been done alone, or in concert with other individuals in fluid affinity groups. The best repudiation of reformism I can figure, at least in terms of a legalistic solution, would be to cancel your voter registration. I proved it worked it Texas, and Shane proved it worked in Illinois, so it is possible to revoke your individual consent to be governed, at least to that extent.

Reformism is a negative externality itself, mainly because it unduly increases opportunity costs by tricking people into thinking that the political means of making money is somehow inexplicably viable for securing individual liberty. This foundational basis for reformism ought to be met with public ridicule, open scorn, and widespread contempt by both patriots and libertarians. At this juncture, the term "activist" might as well mean reformist. Might I suggest that, in order to distinguish ourselves from reformists, patriots and libertarians henceforth describe themselves as freedom outlaws?

Afterword

Readers of The Last Bastille Blog, as well as other content producers within the alternative media, have asked me over the years why I thought this series debunking reformism was indispensably vital to the cause of securing American liberty. Originally, it all began with a conversation I had with none other than Randy Mack of You Have Tread on Me Radio, when I told him how much I despised working within the system in order to change it, he replied by telling me that I should look at all the other methods and then turn each of these articles into a series.

Three years later, that's exactly what I've done.

Misinformation and disinformation are lethal to freedom, because they increase opportunity costs. There are people I have known personally who would have used the economic means of making money, but instead opted for the political means, simply because they still believed in the false viability of reformism itself. This anthology was written for them, as much as for anyone else who sincerely cares about human liberty.

To loosely paraphrase Matthew 3:12, we must separate the wheat from the chaff by, first, recognizing the chaff for what it is, casting it into the fire, and then evaluating the remaining varieties of wheat on their own merits.

Some of that chaff which deserves to be mentioned here are those "false friends," whether they be advocates of an Article V convention, or those oath-breaking "Oathkeepers" and "constitutional" sheriffs who might as well be the King's guards. Rewriting the Constitution of 1787 before the many local Committees of Safety have wrested control away from the enemy rebel government is downright foolhardy; and in the interest of peace, I sincerely encourage those Bluecoats to find a more honorable profession before Americans begin using them for target practice.

Six months ago, I published The Restoration Trilogy, so I hope this anthology has convinced you to ditch the ballot and jury boxes alike. It is my sincerest intention that I was able to persuade you into discarding the political means forever.

I agree with Shane; much like how the answer to security theater is security culture, the answer to reformism is, indeed, direct action.

Kyle Rearden
Austin, Texas
July, 2015

Get Kyle's other book, *JUST BELOW THE SURFACE: A GUIDE TO SECURITY CULTURE!*

WWW.LIBERTYUNDERATTACK.COM